FORGIVE THE LANGUAGE

Katy Evans-Bush's poetry publications are *Me and the Dead, Egg Printing Explained* (Salt Publishing, 2008 & 2011) and *Oscar & Henry* (2010, Rack Press). Her blog, *Baroque in Hackney*, was shortlisted for the George Orwell Prize for political writing in 2012. She lives in Stoke Newington, London.

Forgive the
Language

ESSAYS ON POETS & POETRY

Penned in the Margins

LONDON

PUBLISHED BY PENNED IN THE MARGINS
22 Toynbee Studios, 28 Commercial Street, London E1 6AB, United Kingdom
www.pennedinthemargins.co.uk

First published 2015

Printed and bound in the UK by Bell & Bain Ltd, Glasgow

ISBN
978-1-908058-32-4

CONTENTS

ACKNOWLEDGMENTS

We ride on each other's shoulders. This book has been brought into being with the support and at the instigation of a great many people. Essays contained here originally appeared (sometimes in a slightly different form) in the following publications: *The Contemporary Poetry Review* (cprw.com), *The Dark Horse, Horizon Review, Little Atoms, The Los Angeles Review of Books, Magma*, the *Magma* blog, *The Poem* (thepoem.co.uk), *Poetry London, The Poetry Review, Verse Palace*, and my own blog, *Baroque in Hackney*.

I thank the editors who commissioned, worked with, and sometimes improved these essays: Edward Barker, Charles Boyle, Gerry Cambridge, Tom Chivers, Tim Dooley, Ernest Hilbert, Jane Holland, Frances Leviston, Rob Mackenzie. Additional editorial input, feedback, and research has come from John Clegg, Mark Granier, Tom Lucas (the Typewriter Man), David Secombe, Mike Sims, and Allen Stone, for lending me the Petit.

'The Line' was originally written for Frances Leviston's *Verse Palace*. In a much expanded form it appeared in the anthology *Stress Fractures*, published by Penned in the Margins.

Moral support comes in many forms and has come abundantly over the years from many, many people. First: Michael Donaghy, without whom none of this. Among others: Ruth Fainlight, Naomi Jaffa, Michael Symmons Roberts, Christopher Reid, Don Paterson, Don Share, and Andy Ching. Blogging is hard work too. *Baroque in Hackney* has been partly kept going over the years by moral support and feedback from others — especially Lee Bradshaw, Kristin Heimark, the late Norman Geras, and Suzanne Moore. Thanks to Miles Jupp and Rachel Boase for their brilliant hospitality at the crucial moment. Thanks always, of course, to David Secombe, for his unwavering belief, ideas, prods, stern edits, words, love, and war on exclamation marks.

The title of this book is borrowed from Ian Duhig's poem 'Charivari'. Many thanks.

FOR
GIVE
THE
LANG
UAGE

For Mom

& I.M. Thomas Vink-Lainas
1943-2015

You've got to know the rules to break them. That's what I'm here for, to demolish the rules but keep the tradition.
Alexander McQueen, Savage Beauty, V&A, 2015

THE HIDDEN LIFE OF POETS

Poetry. At first it's all around us, in nursery rhymes, 'children's poems', at primary school, even in some form on children's television. We learn to speak in rhyme, which is patterned language, and it makes up our earliest games. It's at school. Then it becomes something we 'ought' to do. It's homework. Teachers tell us if we got it right or wrong. We move on.

Poetry is the book your boring aunt gives your sister, maybe, and, maybe, your sister hates it. She wants a giant Teletubbies make-up set instead, and everyone agrees it's really *bo-oring*. From this chance moment, perhaps — the moment you quietly take the book to your room, and know nobody will never miss it — poetry is your secret.

At secondary school, poetry rears its head again, but very much in public. 'What do you think the poet is really trying to say here?' 'Can you interpret the symbolism in the metaphor?' 'Analyse the influences of the Metaphysicals on the conceits of...' Oh, wait. 'Where does the real message of 'The Hitcher' come out?'

It's happening in public, but the real poem is still happening in private. You write the stuff in secret. You read it and print it out and keep it in folders, and gradually you show some of your poems to your friends. They say nice things, but what do they know? And maybe they were the ones who laughed at your boring aunt's book with your sister. So it's still — the work that poetry is doing inside you and your conception of language as a medium through which to perceive the world — a big, fat secret.

This essay could be pages and pages long. But ultimately, there is a point for all of us where there is one big difference between our poems and the ones in books. They get read by people, and ours don't. They are written TO be read. The poets who write them do so knowing that they are making something for other people to read, and we write ours both from and to the inside of our head.

Don Paterson talks about the various stages of 'publication' as being the biggest transformation in a poem. He says that in one sense a poem is 'published' — broadcast to the outside world — the minute we show it to someone else. Then there's sharing it in a workshop or an email. Then maybe getting it in a magazine. At each remove, the poem becomes the property of (more) other people, not just us.

This of course changes the poem, because it becomes a public artefact, an object to be used, consumed, participated in, by anyone who finds it. And it changes you, because you now have a different relationship to your secret. It has a perfectly acceptable public side.

With this comes a change in how you write your poems. You need to learn to access both the side that's secret within you, and the side that faces outwards: a strange mysterious element that makes your poem A Thing, Made for Other People. Your innermost thoughts aren't much good to them unless framed in a way they can access, empathise their way into, relate back to the world THEY are perceiving, and — with luck — be surprised by.

This is the life cycle of a poet. The hidden life — that secret that made you steal your sister's Christmas present, and the reason you alone ever noticed that it was not on the shelf where it got dumped — carries on. But the poems you make out of that self begin to have a life of their own, beyond you. They have relationships with other people you might think you have nothing in common with whatever. This is about being human.

A poem works on this level in proportion to what it gives to the reader. General reflections of sagacity, or complicated abstract metaphors about your inner turmoil, are not news; everybody has those. In making a poem for people to read, you are holding something up to the light and saying: "Look! Look at this!" Make sure the reader can *see* what you're holding up; make it come into *their* space a little, and touch them. Let it *ask* them something, not just tell them all about you. Let it sit there so they can just *be* with it.

This means making sure it's clear what the poem is about. Putting specific images in, not just Big Ideas. Not bombarding them with how *you* feel, but creating a space where they can feel it *with* you. It means making sure the images all hang together, the examples all tell the same story, the language fits the mood, the rhymes aren't overpowering.

For many people, the first step out of their hidden life — the first time their secret is aired outside their circle of friends — is sending a poem to a magazine: maybe a local one, or maybe a big, important one which they'll never get in. For some, the first step is sending it to a competition. This feels safe, it's all anonymous, you don't have to have a name. Your secret identity is still secret!

The poem doesn't get anywhere, of course, in this competition. Except that sometimes it does; because it's about the poem, not the poet. But in any case, what it HAS done is this: it's gone and sat in a box with hundreds, maybe thousands, of other poems, all of them poems together, all coming out of the secret space and blinking into the sunshine of an unknown, real *reader*. And maybe, when you think of it sitting in there, you begin to really want your poem to be read by that reader, to be understood, to resonate with them the way other poems have resonated with you. To be, like Pinocchio, alive.

This is an important moment for your poem and for you. It's the moment the lights come on, and shine into your hidden life. You find you are sitting at the beginning of a road...

THE POEM IS A QUESTION:
KEATS, NEGATIVE CAPABILITY AND US

A long time ago, I was trying to write a poem. I'd had a bad evening — a strange bad evening — with a guy I shouldn't have been having anything to do with, and I wanted to write about it. But it wouldn't come right. I was feeling confused and upset, and didn't know what I thought, much less where to start trying to say it. It was a swirling jumble of feelings, impressions and self-justification. After several false starts I thought I'd take some notes, just to get the facts straight. By taking notes I might arrive at what I thought. I said to myself: *Just say what happened.* So I began:

> When you get to the pub you're already drunk —
> You've been down the old Globe or somewhere
> Since lunchtime, and when you come in
> You throw your phone down on the table
>   And start by picking a fight with Jan...
> You're questioning my eye-witness account
> Of a crash that happened outside the office —
> A man just gunned his car at the railing,
> Right into someone — and not by accident —
> And subsequent riot (this very statement
> I note the police believed outright,
> And even wrote it down), while you breathe
> All over me, and fondle my arm.
> You drawl, *I'm playing the devil's advocate.*

Every time I got stuck in the notes, or wasn't sure what I should write next, I thought: *Just say what happened.* When I got to the end of the notes, I suddenly realised that the last thing that happened —

> So then I walk the two miles to work,
> Which gives me time to think — and you know,
> I kind of wish things were different.
> I'm fishing around for my keys in my bag
> When I notice the bloodstains still on the pavement.

— mirrored the first; and what I had thought was a list was in fact a series of lines; and that the notes *were* the poem, and it told me what I was feeling. The incident had taken care of itself, had done its own work in this poem. I called it, ironically, 'The Crash (A Love Letter)'.

Write what you know. That's what we hear. Even schoolchildren are given this advice, whose whole job in the world is to be curious and find everything out. But how do you even know what you know? And really, what does anyone know?

The other adage, which crops up even more frequently is this one: *Show, don't tell.* Generations of writers have been given this advice. Presumably it applies after the writer has figured out what they do and don't know. Once you've figured out what you're writing about, *Show, don't tell* works — right up to the moment when it doesn't.

What it 'means', of course, is that the writer should use concrete nouns ('no ideas but in things,' said William Carlos Williams) instead of abstractions (of which Ezra Pound told poets to 'go in fear'). Modernism taught us to rely on images, which we are told are things we can see (but tell that to Pound, who called an image 'an emotional and intellectual complex in an instant of time'), instead of ideas (and tell *that* to Wallace Stevens).

What I propose, for the good of literature and writers of all ages and backgrounds, is to turn both of these cosy little notions on their heads, and instead tell our young people:

1. Write what you don't know.
2. Ask, don't tell.

It's perfectly safe: they will naturally filter their questions and their doubts through what they *do* know, so no one will be hurt.

In 1817, Keats wrote a letter to his brothers, who had gone to America. His letters were long and chatty, and combined gossip, familial concern, news, and his thoughts about what he was working on, as well as reading. This one contained a small paragraph that comes down to us now like a small meteor, or a magic crystal. He wrote:

'...at once it struck me what quality went to form a Man of Achievement, especially in Literature, and which Shakespeare possessed so enormously — I mean Negative Capability, that is, when a man is capable of being in uncertainties, mysteries, doubts, without any irritable reaching after fact and reason...'

Negative Capability. Careers have been based on defining this phrase, and this was the only time he used it.

One website (keatsian.co.uk) has this interesting thing to say about Negative Capability:

This description can be compared to a definition of conflict: 'An emotional state characterized by indecision, restlessness, uncertainty and tension resulting from incompatible inner needs or drives of comparable intensity'.

These two definitions are very similar; the meaning of conflict sounds very negative and hopeless. However, Keats' creative concept seems positive and full of potential by leaving out 'restlessness' and avoiding an 'irritable reaching after fact and reason'.

In another letter, Keats says that the 'poetical character... has no self — it is everything and nothing — it has no character and enjoys light and shade; it lives in gusto, be it foul or fair, high or low, rich or poor, mean or elevated — it has as much delight in conceiving an Iago as an Imogen. [...] A Poet is the most unpoetical of anything in existence, because he has no identity, he is continually filling some other body.'

The essay mentions the idea of 'not imposing one self upon the doubts and uncertainties which make up a conflict', and goes on:

> The word 'doubt' is from the Latin, 'dubitare' and comes from 'two' as in two minds. In most conflicts, two people (i.e. two minds) oppose each other. Yet instead of fighting the other, Keats finds the situation to be one that is open for creativity.

So, Negative Capability is not about a capability as such, and it isn't about being 'negative'. The phrase can possibly be understood in the light of two other ways in which we use the word 'negative'. One of them is the photographic negative — which contains all the information necessary for the picture, but does not yet present it — and the other is the concept of negative space. That is the space that surrounds the subject of the picture; it's everything except the thing you think you're looking at, and it defines the thing you're looking at. If all you are doing is 'telling' about' or 'showing' the thing you think you're looking at, you are missing (as Keats seems to be telling us) most of the information.

The other thing that makes the term confusing is this word:

capability. Nowadays we would be more likely to call it a capacity. It's a capacity for sitting in the moment (but it's a moment that encompasses all other moments); for effacing our own observing, classifying, self-oriented ego and sitting open to frequencies that we may not understand. This is not the same as 'mindfulness'; it's more about getting past your mind.

TS Eliot's essay 'Tradition and the Individual Talent' addresses the same idea. This is the essay where the famous quote originates, that: 'Poetry is not a turning loose of emotion, but an escape from emotion; it is not the expression of personality, but an escape from personality.' This begins to come to it, but there is something more specific, nuanced, and pertinent earlier on in the essay:

> ...the poet has, not a 'personality' to express, but a particular medium, which is only a medium and not a personality, in which impressions and experiences combine in peculiar and unexpected ways. Impressions and experiences which are important for the man may take no place in the poetry, and those which become important in the poetry may play quite a negligible part in the man, the personality.

Shakespeare crops up in Keats' paragraph; he also appears in Eliot's essay. It is Negative Capability or something like it that Eliot is referring to when he says, 'Shakespeare acquired more essential history from Plutarch than most men could from the whole British Museum'. One might call it the ability to extrapolate with intuition.

Robert Browning, that master of other people's voices and their self-delusions, is quoted in the website above: 'I walk, I behold that that I can be and become anything I look at and reach an understanding'. And in a line from *To the Lighthouse*, Virginia Woof wrote: 'Mrs Ramsay looked intently until she became the things she looked upon.' This seems to get at something. It certainly would, if

Mrs Ramsay were a writer; what Woolf has done here is give Mrs Ramsay her own capacity.

If we approach the idea of Negative Capability from these angles, we begin to see that 'looking intently' in this way is less about already knowing the thing than it is about being open to the thing, about clearing space inside so you can absorb it — and definitely more like asking about it than telling about it.

As writers, we can regard a poem, almost any poem, as an act of questioning. This is in line with Don Paterson's remark that for poets, 'rhyme' is a verb, not a noun. If we accept that a poem is an act of questioning, then the world can be treated as a question, and you, the poet, act as the question mark. The answer to the question is arrived at through the medium of complete openness. This is not extinction of the personality, as in a squashing or suppressing; it's more like a thinning of it which enables it to absorb and contain other things.

There's another state of uncertainties and doubts a person can be in, and learn to occupy, of course; that's a state we tend to pathologise nowadays as 'depression' — which people used to call 'melancholy'. Keats himself was prone to the condition and wrote one of his greatest poems on the subject, in doing so epitomising his Negative Capability in action. The poem was a means of enacting a question — or that irritable reaching — and overcoming it:

> No, no, go not to Lethe, neither twist
>   Wolf's-bane, tight-rooted, for its poisonous wine;
> Nor suffer thy pale forehead to be kiss'd
>   By nightshade, ruby grape of Proserpine...

This poem begins *in media res*, with an answer: 'No. no, go not to Lethe'. So there is a question, hanging modestly in the background.

And the poet is still asking it even as he goes into fantastic detail, describing its many permutations. You might say the question is something like: *How do I live with this?*

Note how Keats never talks about his own feelings. But he certainly has these feelings, because otherwise he couldn't write, 'But when the melancholy fit shall fall/ Sudden from heaven like a weeping cloud'; if he didn't, he couldn't give such detailed instructions for encompassing the torment. He makes a startling exhortation to 'feed deep, deep' on the anger in one's lover's eyes, right after the instruction to 'glut' one's sorrow — and then goes on:

> She dwells with Beauty—Beauty that must die;
>   And Joy, whose hand is ever at his lips
> Bidding adieu; and aching Pleasure nigh,
>   Turning to poison while the bee-mouth sips:
> Ay, in the very temple of Delight
>   Veil'd Melancholy has her sovran shrine...

This is the crux, the place from which the contradictions emanate. And he still goes on — saying that only those who can experience true joy can even appreciate the shrine — i.e., the place of worship — of this mysterious veiled goddess. And that their souls will be given to her as 'cloudy trophies'. And that's if you can experience joy! This is living with(in) the contradiction.

Notice again that first line: 'No no...' In everything exists its opposite. So Keats is clearly imagining, and inviting the reader to imagine, a scenario where he's said 'Yes, yes...' Yes, go to Lethe, go to sleep, take the opium, dull your senses. Let the shades come to you, as they certainly will if you make yourself a shade.

Two hundred years later and in a different register completely, another poem that appears to embody Negative Capability is Philip Gross' 'Elderly Iceberg off the Esplanade', from his collection, *Water Table* (Bloodaxe, 2010).

> Last night it came knocking, a first
> since the end of the Ice Age. A stray eddy brought it,
> a backhander from the Gulf Stream. It was heading
>   inland, could it be to spawn?
>
> It had jumped ship from the loosening Arctic,
> was a waster, pock-marked, sunken-featured,
> in its mud mac. Lurked in the sea lane, only wanted love.
>   Was a monster, unnaturally born...

The poem goes about observing this iceberg, giving it a set of qualities, then another, then another: 'unassuming little thing'; 'huge/ in no definite sense'; 'past help, on the edge of extinction'. It's a state of very active imaginative observation — something that can't happen if you already think you know what you'll see.

> ...It wasn't the last,
> just a message from lastness, a crumpled
> brown parcel from an unsuspected
>   awful aunt who might
>
> just turn up any day to stay. Naturally
> it was impossible; such things have to be
> believed...
>
> ... Let it go.
> This world should not detain it.
>   It would do the same for you.

It's impressive how much empathy Gross applies to this iceberg, how he reels in his effects. Observed and described, characterised, the iceberg never becomes anything but an iceberg (except symbolically); it never becomes anthropomorphic. It is thoroughly an iceberg.

There are questions, suppositions, changes of view here: it's a poem of working-out. Look at how the stanzas enact that *dubitare* sense of things described above, accommodating conflicts, and how the final line hangs off the end of each one — perhaps like an iceberg. Even the half-sentence, 'Call it a bad dream/ if you like', contains two provisional qualifications, and these are followed by evidence-gathering: 'when I looked this morning'... The stanza after this contains three negatives about one small word: silt. The last line of the poem is all the more shocking for being actually reasonable. It arrives as a conclusion, not a destination.

A poem can be said to have two phases, or two obvious ones among many. One is the process of its making, where it's all contingent, in draft, not yet together in its pieces; the other is its existence as a made object, which exists as something whole, inevitable, immutable. One belongs to the poet, and one to itself — and to the reader. When a poem has attained the second state it should be feasible for the poet to answer a questioner in the manner of Harold Pinter: 'It's in the text'. It is something a person can read and — at least emotionally — comprehend.

I'm using that last word 'comprehend' in its sense of, not 'understand', but 'encompass'. A student of mine once addressed this issue, saying, 'I'm making assumptions about poems I really like — assuming that they knew where they were going when they were in the process of writing.' But uncertainty is the basis of everything that's any good. The author knew the story but not how to achieve all its stages. The poet knew the last line but now how to get to it. The writer knew something but not how to say it. The point was polemic but images and metaphors suggested themselves. The poet listened.

The made poem, in its second phase, operates on both the inside, where the working-out took place, and on the outside, as an artefact being presented to the world. On the inside, the poet has been open to minute vibrations, symbol, and multiple meanings — like a spider's web or satellite dish. And the outside is like the hard carapace. The signals have been filtered. Meaning has been snapped into place, shaping the material to suggest answers to the questions.

I often think of an interview James Stewart gave, about his big drunk scene in *The Philadelphia Story*. In this scene he is crashingly, excitedly, incredibly drunkenly drunk, and goes to see Cary Grant. He's a bit in love with Katharine Hepburn and is also a journalist in possession of a great story. It's totally exhilarating, completely and joyously convincing. The interviewer asked Stewart: how did you do it? Stewart said it had struck him that when actors go to play a drunk man, they tend to try to act drunk; but that every drunk man is trying to act sober.

I also read, a while ago, an interview with Tom Stoppard in which he said: 'most people have a misapprehension that a play comes out of an idea, whereas 'in reality the idea comes out of the play'. The article went on, 'He acknowledges how powerful theatre with a message can be, but "a play works or doesn't work on an emotional level".'

This is a big arrow pointing us towards what needs to be contained or encompassed within a poem:

⇨   THAT WHICH WILL HELP THE READER FEEL EMOTIONAL TRUTH

Not the poet's daily emotions, as we have seen above, but the significant, depersonalised, poetically realised emotion.

Michael Donaghy, in his workshops, used to hold his

cupped hand up, as if he were holding a globe. "Alas, poor Yorick!", he'd tell the class. This was his physical shorthand for the quality of urgency, that the poem about showing something to the reader. "Look!" it says. As he stood there, the invisible globe in his hand became a skull, and each still-unwritten poem became a matter of life and death.

Comic or tragic, larger than life or a tiny moment, and even if it's ('just') a play on language – a successful poem creates the curiosity that feeds it and inspires an emotional hunger, however fragmentary or momentary, in the reader. Something is at stake. The poet serves this best by getting out of the way, even if writing about his or her own life. It's about the work. There is another arrow here:

⇨ CREATIVITY IS A PROCESS OF SUBTRACTION

The subtraction is of the reaching after fact and reason – the explanations, the judgements, the announcements of feeling, the false feeling, received wisdom, the didactic assumptions arrived at before the poem has been fully written (or even started). This stuff is just static. 'The idea comes out of the play'. Even if the poet knows the idea – has an idea – at the beginning of the composition process, it must, by the end, be expressed *through* – not just in – the poem itself.

Openness, with control. Creative writing books often refer to the control part of the writing brain as the 'inner editor', usually with an injunction to ignore it. But a poet in a state of negative capability – 'capable of being in uncertainties, mysteries, doubts, without any irritable reaching after fact and reason' – can use this openness to arrive at a sense of the final shape and emotional content of the poem, and to begin to shape it quietly with one part of the brain while 'taking dictation' with the other. These two minds are both the poet: one is receiving, one is filtering. One is asking, one is seeing. One is gathering, one is making. Neither is concerned with the poet's 'personality' or with a (literally) preconceived idea.

If Negative Capability is negative in the sense of a photographic negative, then, as in a darkroom, one can see an image emerging from the information stored in the draft. Here is a moment for 'entering the spirit of the observed', to finish the image.

Elizabeth Bishop's poem 'Cirque d'Hiver' is an extraordinary compressed moment of observation:

> Across the floor flits the mechanical toy,
> fit for a king of several centuries back.
> A little circus horse with real white hair.
> His eyes are glossy black.
> He bears a little dancer on his back.

The minute description in this poem is framed within a very tight stanza structure whose deceptively delicate rhymes form an inescapable rhetorical thrust. The repetition mimics the little circles in which the toy repetitively moves: 'She stands upon her toes and turns and turns./ A slanting spray of artificial roses/ is stitched across her skirt and tinsel bodice'.

In the third stanza, a surprise: 'He has a formal, melancholy soul'... More than this, 'He feels her pink toes dangle toward his back/ along the little pole/ that pierces both her body and her soul'. It is quite possible to imagine that Bishop didn't even see this coming, till it came. In the final line of stanza four the poem abruptly ascends to a new level:

> He canters three steps, then he makes a bow,
> canters again, bows on one knee,

canters, then clicks and stops, and looks at me.

This is a massive jolt of consciousness. Suddenly we are aware of the observer. In fact, it's no longer just observation; it's confrontation. Think how much more effective Bishop's treatment is than if she had begun the poem — which she would never do, of course — by saying something like, 'I'm looking at a mechanical toy...'

'He is the more intelligent by far'. The dancer cannot be relied on for anything. She turns away. In the final stanza the sudden interchange becomes complete, desperation is acknowledged, and the emotional content explodes — like a star — leaving you, along with Elizabeth Bishop, in a place you could never have imagined at the beginning.

I've never seen a draft of this poem, but you can see that the finished version contains all the emotional information needed to *feel* the content, and nothing that does not serve the emotional or cognitive understanding of it. At the same time, it masquerades as (mere) observation. It acts itself out, like a play where the idea originates and is expressed through the action, where the *dubitare* — the horse and the dancer, the horse and Elizabeth, the horse and the reader — is the propulsive force, where the symbol is part of the action, where the language is part of the symbol, where nothing can be taken out.

When I quoted Keats's letter at the start of this essay, telling his brothers about his idea of Negative Capability, I didn't include the sentence immediately after, where he complains that Coleridge, for example, doesn't have it. Always trying to say what the thing is, always irritably reaching after fact and reason. (Maybe this is where the opium came in, so susceptible to sudden visitors.) There are undoubtedly more writers who achieved a great deal without being able to rise above their own personalities; it could make an amusing parlour game, spotting them. Wordsworth, for example, kept fussing with 'THE PRELUDES' all his life, making little irritable changes that bowdlerised his original vision. He couldn't tolerate the frequencies, not just from other people, but even from his earlier self.

It reminds me of the little sign with a clip-art man on it that I've seen taped to the wall above so many poets' desks: 'You don't have to have Negative Capability to work here, but it helps'.

JAMES MERRILL, FORMAL RADICAL

Mention James Merrill in the UK and you will quite probably draw a blank face. Even with a Pulitzer Prize and both a Collected Prose and Collected Poetry published by Knopf in the US, he remains little read here. If your listener has heard of him, their response is likely to be delivered in that polite voice we reserve for conversations about someone's sick relative. Merrill was a major poet of the American 20th century, with a dazzling linguistic fluidity and a refined and buoyant wit. But against the tide of let-it-all-hang-out, confessionalist, accessible, beat, Yippie, 'democratised', surrealist, fractured, post-Modernist, insert-label-here poetry, he stands out mostly as that thing we call Mandarin. His style, like that of Fred Astaire, has gone out of fashion — except, of course, among us for whom it hasn't.

Meanwhile, metrical poetry has had a bad rap over the past seventy years or so, and nowhere more than in America. Rhyme has come off badly, with most poets simply preferring, like Bartleby, not to. Things are a little better here in the UK, but even so there is that sort of almost inflectionless, polite free-verse voice that renders so many new collections rather... samey. Except among 'formalists'. And formalists can be more than a bit samey too. Movements like The Movement in the British 1950s, or the New Formalists of the American 1980s, have gathered round a rather conservative aesthetic (and in some cases, a conservative politics, which only eggs on all the hippies who think that rhyme or pattern is somehow 'hierarchical' or 'elitist' — as if all children didn't learn to talk by playing with rhyme) — as if all poets in the past had written in the style of Thomas Hardy.

Asked what he thought about the New Formalists, Michael Donaghy would reply, "The old formalists never went away". Along with Anthony Hecht and Richard Wilbur, or (say) Keats or Coleridge, he was referring here to James Merrill.

In reality, of course, when poets in the past churned out those old-fashioned versified poems, they were figuring it out for themselves. Every great poet from the past is great precisely because they (in Pound's words) made it new. They solved their technical problems from scratch: Donne, Milton, Byron, Blake, Dickinson. They were all, to that extent, radical. Creating only the art that *only you* could possibly create is something not many do. The world doesn't require it and mostly doesn't even want it, and most practising artists have no idea what that thing only *they* can do might be.

Merrill has an extra problem in the American poetry scene. Not only was he a formalist; he was also terribly, terribly rich. As the son of Charles Merrill, co-founder of the Merrill-Lynch firm, he floated through life on a trust fund so capacious that he asked his accountant not even to tell him his income: he never spent near it. Merrill was sent to Arizona aged six, after the Lindbergh baby's kidnapping, lest he might be at risk. He was an opera-lover from the age of 12; he travelled Europe in a Jamesian mode, and bought a house in Athens, where for many years he spent half his time. He utterly eschewed politics. His central influence was Proust; he wrote about his parents' high-society divorce, and his relationship with his governess. He was rich and terribly, un-Americanly, highbrow.

But lives are more complex than bank statements; Merrill was a misfit. On the most obvious level, he was a gay man born in 1926, who spent his whole life trying to reconcile his need to live (and write) honestly with the considerable pressures of society (beginning with his mother). He was able to buy himself the freedom of distance, and also to make the financial accommodations necessary to free his long-term partner up for travelling, living in Greece, etc. These travels informed not only the cast of characters in his work, but also his idiosyncratic symbolic iconography: the kimono, for example, after which one of his most famous poems is titled.

And below the obvious level, he was much more than just a rich, clever man. His stature doesn't come from these biographical facts. They are incidental, except insofar as the money enabled the life, which enabled and informed the writing. James Merrill was not only a consummate stylist, who wrote straight out of language itself – his poetry was luminously sophisticated, elegant, funny, and multi-layered – he was a deep and serious thinker about poetry, and out of a rather glittering social pool he drew darkly lit, real, difficult wisdom. Almost any poem you can read by Merrill will take you to a place you weren't expecting, and make you look at yourself again. He wrote, like Proust, about his everyday life, memory, his childhood – with its recurring motifs of mirrors, red setters, jigsaws, ghosts, palms, love – and until the 1970s he managed to do this without being very openly gay.

The criticisms of Merrill are familiar: chilly, patrician, arch, decorative. James Dickey called his 1959 collection, *The Country of a Thousand Years of Peace*, 'a realm of connoisseurish aesthetic contemplation', and described it as 'enough to drive you mad over the needless artificiality, prim finickiness, and determined inconsequence of it all'.

This was to miss the point and, anyway, Merrill was ready to loosen up his style. He had made friends with the New York school poets in the early 1950s. Their freewheeling approach was not, ultimately, for him; he needed lightness, yes, but also more sheer language, more virtuosity, more chiaroscuro, than they could muster. He shared with them the desire to write naturally and freely about life, but he needed to find his own way.

Like Proust, he fictionalised his life into art. Another great inspiration, Wallace Stevens, allowed him to be, as he said Stevens was, both 'grand *and* playful' (as he told JD McClatchy in his *Paris Review* interview) — 'combining abstract words and gaudy visual or sound effects', creating a physical atmosphere as foil, or as Eliot's 'objective correlative', for the emotional or spiritual content beneath it.

This is the entire basis of his major work, *The Changing Light at Sandover* — a three-book epic based on Merrill's 20-year adventure with a Ouija board, that has 'the glitz and wackiness of Broadway, the erudition of the *New York Times* Science Supplement, and the social sophistication of Henry James', as John Greening wrote ('Ouija: The poetry of James Merrill (1926-1995)', *The Dark Horse*, 2010). It's a mad, one-of-a-kind poem that stands alone in 20th century letters. In one sense it's a domestic poem, with Merrill and his partner David Jackson sitting at the board or going about their lives. It's also a saga of the Afterlife, the Other World, and its concerns are celestial and eternal. It's a sprawling work —'(almost as long as *Paradise Lost!*)'.

The cast of characters includes Ephraim, a sweet Jewish slave from the palace of Caligula, for whom the first book is named; a tribe of talking bats; and a dizzying array of deceased friends, DJ's parents, and poets. Yeats and Wallace Stevens both make appearances, and, most notably, Auden — who, as Merrill's biographer, Langdon Hammer, points out, is closest to being Merrill's poetic alter ego. The second book, *Mirabell: Books of Number*, is almost more like science fiction or some religious cult involving numerology, the 'God of Biology', and the talking bats. The three books make up a record: of a relationship, of the minutiae of daily life, of innumerable conversations, of ideas that range from preposterous to erudite to madcap. As it happens, they also contain sudden passages of beauty and ineffable wisdom about life and death, in the way a swimming pool will suddenly drop from three to six feet; the bottom just disappears beneath you.

As Greening says, the poem demanded of Merrill 'every conceivable formal device'. The speech of the spirits, based on transcripts that Merrill wrote during the seances, is rendered in capital letters, giving the poem a strange look on the page, like scientific text, code or poison pen letters. Its three books are structured after the elements of the Ouija board itself: *The Book of Ephraim* has 26 sections based on the letters of the alphabet; *Mirabell*'s sections are numbered 0-9, and *Scripts for the pageant* is based on the words YES and NO. In terms of form, the poem looks rambling and loose, but it is highly intricate. Greening wrote that this epic work:

> offered [Merrill] a chance to shine at everything: to adopt voices, to try on genres and discard them, to lecture or sing, converse or debate, to create characters or to be confessional, to tell a story or to philosophise, to play games or to ask the big questions.

The Changing Light at Sandover is the central work of Merrill's career, but it grows directly out of the same concerns that formed his other work: memory, time, people, love, death, the nature of wisdom, the nature of existence. It's full of mirrors and seeing — or not-seeing.

One of my favourite poems — a small thing, from Merrill's 1966 collection, *Nights and Days*, called 'Charles on Fire' — encapsulates many of the qualities of Merrill's work, like one of those tiny demonstration cupboards made by journeymen carpenters. In less than a page this poem packs in double meanings, changes in tone, several frames of reference, social comedy, dialogue, fire, an idea of the afterlife, and a mirror.

> Another evening we sprawled about discussing
> Appearances. And it was the consensus

That while uncommon physical good looks
Continued to launch one, as before, in life
(Among its vaporous eddies and false claims),
Still, as one of us said into his beard,
"Without your intellectual and spiritual
Values, man, you are sunk." No one but squared
The shoulders of their own unlovliness.
Long-suffering Charles, having cooked and served the meal,
Now brought out little tumblers finely etched
He filled with amber liquor and then passed.
"Say," said the same young man, "in Paris, France,
They do it this way"--bounding to his feet
And touching a lit match to our host's full glass.
A blue flame, gentle, beautiful, came, went
Above the surface. In a hush that fell
We heard the vessel crack. The contents drained
As who should step down from a crystal coach.
Steward of spirits, Charles's glistening hand
All at once gloved itself in eeriness.
The moment passed. He made two quick sweeps and
Was flesh again. "It couldn't matter less,"
He said, but with a shocked, unconscious glance
Into the mirror. Finding nothing changed,
He filled a fresh glass and sank down among us.

The texture of this poem is characteristically both rich and light; indeed the surroundings are rich and light, with a dinner, guests and candles. The story is simple. A couple of exchanges and then an accident, and a small moment when everything is, for a second, out of the ordinary. It's such a small moment, and the transformation is so thorough, that it's hard even to tell it. Just look at the words that crop up, symbolic, visual, carrying double meanings or associations. We have 'appearances', 'life', 'vaporous', the archaic 'unlovliness', 'little tumblers finely etched', 'amber liquor', the match, 'above the surface'. Then comes this amazing moment:

> We heard the vessel crack. The contents drained
> As who should step down from a crystal coach.
> Steward of spirits, Charles's glistening hand
> All at once gloved itself in eeriness.

The vessel. Steward of spirits. This poem pre-dates *Sandover* by years, but it was written a decade after 'Voices From Another World', Merrill's first attempt at the Ouija material. What is really draining from that glass? Even 'etched' calls to mind the 'mezzotint' of an earlier dinner-party poem, 'A Narrow Escape': an anecdote about a guest who cheerfully announces herself to be a vampire. With the references to Cinderella (and her pumpkin), the suggested vampire and even the 'spirits', these lines contain a whole European culture's-worth of contingency, transfiguration and identity shift.

Then that line break, all the suspense turning on that hairpin: 'and / Was flesh again'. And then the mirror. By this stage in the poem it's reassuring to know that Charles could see his reflection. He finds 'nothing changed', but in reality everything has changed. Something called normality returned, 'he filled a fresh glass', but he 'sank down' (drained) among us.

As Merrill told McClatchy: 'the phrasing leads to the content. I don't really know how to separate those'. This is a cousin of Don Paterson's oft-repeated statement that sound is meaning, that the two are interchangeable. So if you read Merrill's 'phrasing' as in the musical sense, looking at the rhythm of lines, placement of words and sounds for tempo, the tonal colours, and shifts of key, you can see how a poem like 'Charles on Fire' is impossible to paraphrase. Language, for him, exists specifically to be able to say more than one thing at a time. 'A lot of what we're loosely calling "meaning",' he told McClatchy, turns out, on inspection, to be metaphor, which leads one back toward language: wordplay, etymology, the "wholly human instrument" (as Wystan says) I'd used and trusted — like every poet, wouldn't you say? — to ground the lightning of ideas'. The artist he reminds me of the most is Mozart, the way he weaves his themes together with comic or grotesque touches, and little homilies, and then all of a sudden you are plunged into a moment of the most sublime, almost unbearable purity, it's like eternity. (Speaking of which, he remarked of Blake's famous line that 'you don't see eternity *except* in the grain of sand'.)

So James Merrill committed the radical act of being a consummate artist and a great technician. His poems, even those that a casual reader might think looked too easy, conversational, like free verse, are meticulously built. His formal structures, that of Sandover or that of Charles on Fire — or the sonnets that go together to make 'The Broken Home', the cryptic riddle of 'The Kimono', the densely interwoven puns, symbols and mysteries of 'Lost in Translation', or the half a Christmas tree in his eponymous poem about impending death — operate like the bicycles in Michael Donaghy's poem 'Machines': 'which only by moving can balance, and only by balancing move'.

COMPENDIUM IN TIME

ADVENTURES IN FORM, EDITED BY TOM CHIVERS
(PENNED IN THE MARGINS, 2012)
ON POETRY, GLYN MAXWELL (OBERON BOOKS, 2012)

The Shakers, that celibate American sect famous for their simple, beautiful furniture and textiles, had a saying: 'Every force evolves a form'. This speaks of two things: one, a fundamental respect for the integrity of the made object. And two, an understanding of the kinetic, the physical, origins of its making; in fact, of its transition from idea to object.

In the beginning the force was exerted.

Dai Vaughan, the distinguished film editor and writer who died a couple of years ago, had a little piece of paper pinned up over his desk that said: 'Form is love'.

Think about that.

With the books under review here, two powerful kinetic forces in British poetry have exerted their force on the notion of 'form'. We're long overdue a serious consideration of form (which is, after all, only the opposite of 'chaos') that looks beyond the tired saw of rhyming/metrical vs not-rhyming/metrical. 'Form' has for ages somehow been seen as a sort of veneer, something that's tacked on to make some kind of point, as if there were nothing left under the surface of postmodernism. An interest in structure has been enough to label someone 'conservative', as if it were a political matter.

When I was 13, my mother called me down to the kitchen and told me to watch something on TV; it was *The Importance of Being Earnest,* and it threw me somewhat. But when she said afterwards that it was 'a triumph of form over function', I can remember replying: 'What do you mean? Form *makes* it function; the form *is* the function'. Precocious, maybe. But it's still a radical position.

Tom Chivers, publisher of Penned in the Margins, has edited a commensurately radical anthology of poems showing 'how form can be employed as a framework for innovation'; intending it to act as 'a bestiary of exotic textual creatures'. In it, poems by 46 poets — from arch-experimentalists like Christian Bök and Theodoros Chiotis to polymaths Ruth Padel and George Szirtes, via Oulipians, epistolarians and various kinds of code — provide a glimpse into a world of poetry teeming with life of all kinds, with a dazzling array of plumage and toothery and mating cries.

There's another quote, from Paul Muldoon: 'Form is a straitjacket the way a straitjacket was a straitjacket for Houdini'. So *Adventures in Form* is, among other things, a compendium of daring escapes.

Glyn Maxwell's book *On Poetry* seems, in contrast, a quiet enough thing. It's intensely personal — a sort of combination teaching guide, polemic and discursive philosophy of what poetry is, in particular what form is — and what it's for. But don't be fooled: it's as highly charged as a stick of poetry dynamite, blowing everything out and starting again from first principles. The first two chapters are called 'White' and 'Black'.

'Let's start with poetry's inventions that are absolutely required', Maxwell writes, taking a point from Aristotle: 'their names are *something* and *nothing...*'

Poets work with two materials, one's black and one's white. Call them sound and silence, life and death, hot and cold, love and loss; any can be the case but none of these yins and yangs tell the whole story. What you feel the whiteness is *right now* — consciously or more likely some way beneath that plane — will determine what you do next. Call it this and that, whatever it is *this time*, just don't make the mistake of thinking the white sheet is nothing... For a poet it's everything.

For Maxwell, the white is time. In the next chapter, 'Black', he writes:

> In my work the white is everything but me, and the black is me... All I believe, and therefore all I teach... is that the form and tone and pitch of any poem should coherently express the presence of a human creature. Content, matter, subject, these all play little part. Form plays almost every part, which is why I continue to say that who masters form masters time.

This notion of time is integral to the book. The poems, the forms, that last are the ones that move within its elements in what Maxwell calls a 'creaturely' way. The living presence is there on the page, in black and white. Time, he says, is our enemy. Who masters form masters time. And he re-envisages poetry as a synaesthesiac struggle between the black and the white, where the white presses in on the black, shaping it, and the black exerts its force on the white...

> Indent is a form of punctuation, but a white one not a black one. Line- and stanza-break are the same: white punctuation. Any spaces you make on the page, you are dabbling in the element you don't know. So just — know that. Because all punctuation is is a polite request to time.

Which brings us back to *Adventures in Form*, with its creatures crouching in black and white on the field of our own particular time. Both these books are beautifully stripped-back, black-and-white productions, with absolutely says-it-on-the-tin chapter headings: in Maxwell, 'Black', 'White', 'Form', 'Pulse', 'Space', and so on. In *Adventures in Form*, 'Found Materials'; 'Txts, Tweets and Status Updates'; 'N+7'; 'Emergent'; 'Code is Poetry'. In 'Traditional Revised', sonnets and sestinas get the spam and breakbeat treatment (I wish I'd known about this book; I'd have liked to send in some of my spam poems). The book is full of various kinds of sonnets.

Maxwell says, 'Certain forms abide, and it ought to fall to each new generation to master them, rework them for the times. Otherwise they enervate and wither, and you see poets turning back to a kind of defensive formalism born of nostalgia'. (This happened with the Georgians, too; not just the New Formalists.) And so, this book contains at least one cento, a 'found' form that originated in Ancient Rome and was popular during the Renaissance. It has a sestina, several sonnets, a poem in two columns based on Anglo-Saxon alliterative form (though without alliteration), investigations of translation, and an ancient Celtic form updated.

It also contains many poems written in forms that seem to speak more about the poet's process than about the shape of the object — the *force* at work. Randomisers range from classic Oulipo N+7 (now 50 years old) to predictive text messaging, to lines painted on the backs of sheep and rearranged according to where the sheep wandered. Several poets-worth of 'invented' forms, where a poet imposes more and more arcane limitations on himself, demonstrate varying degrees of success. Some of them don't really appear to be forms at all — just poets with some sort of structural rationale. Poems shaped as correspondence don't strike me as a very revolutionary concept (*Pamela*, Samuel Richardson's benchmark epistolary novel, was published about a mile from the Penned in the Margins office, in 1740) and some of these seemed a bit thin — not very *compressed*, as the mainstream crowd might say. The danger, in several sections of the book, is of foregrounding what looks like (but may not really be) novelty. The poem has to outlast the trick of it.

But this book is wonderful and full of delights and challenges. It watches poets — established, young, 'mainstream','experimental' — as they seek to hew something new and meaningful out of the old rock. Out of, as Glyn Maxwell calls the iambic pentameter (which several of these poets write in), 'this magnificent engine of English poetry'. It shows that the choice absolutely isn't about being *either* New Formalist *or* 'without form, and void'. That being experimental, on some terms or other, is common to every poet, to every poem ever written. Even the poems written in — or partly in — computer code are creaturely and poetic — in particular Chris McCabe's 'Recession'. (Many of these poems seem to operate via accumulation and transformation; they're very hard to quote the odd line from.)

Highlights: Chrissy Williams' 'The Lost', made out of various translations of the opening of *The Divine Comedy*; George Ttoouli's haunting 'May Day', from 'Three Warnings'; Paul Muldoon's 'Eating Chinese Food in a Straw Bale House, Snowmass, Colorado, January 2011'; Ross Sutherland's Oulipo Red Riding Hood, 'The Liverish Red-Blooded Riffraff Hooha' (which reminds me of Howard Chace's homophonic jeu d'esprit, 'Ladle Rat Rotten Hut', written in 1940); Paul Stephenson's 'Family Values', a reworking of a potted bio of Carol Vorderman; Simon Barraclough's 'Manifest'; Christian Bök's masterly sequential translation of Rimbaud's 'Voyelles':

> O, the supreme Trumpeter of our strange sonnet —
> quietudes crossed by another [World and Spirit],
> O, the Omega! — the violet raygun of [Her] Eyes...

'Voyelles', by the way, gets a name-check in *On Poetry*, too, in a statement that takes on layers of meaning (like synaesthesiac impressions?) as one continues to think about it:

I'd certainly have failed Arthur Rimbaud for writing that poem called 'Voyelles' in which he calls 'A noir, E blanc, I rouge, U vert, O bleu'. Amateur. Anyone knows it's A yellow, E blue, I white, O black, U purples. What do you think it is? Please don't say. Maybe synaesthesia is something one does alone.

Like the bestiary its editor calls it, *Adventures in Form* teems with life. It is a start towards a new, and healthier, way of looking at the poetic endeavour we live among. As such, it's essential reading right now, and I hope there will be sequels.

As for Glyn Maxwell's book, there are a handful of books *about* writing that I count among my indispensible texts: by Guy Davenport, Randall Jarrell, Durs Grünbein, Keats, Pound, Brodsky, Virginia Woolf, Fanny Burney, Eliot. I knew by page two that this book was one of them.

In the full spirit of Glyn Maxwell's black-on-white creature, here is Hannah Silva conquering time, in her text-speak 'Grecian Urn' poem, 'a mo ina _/ jar':

> ... Go get her m8. &he did.
> Didn't you? As if dat wz it,
> dat simpl. u thort, 1day n d
> fucha der wl B a _/ jar on a
> countA in arm dat l%ks lk
> u n l%ks lk M2n dat jar wl
> contain ll deez moments,
> n d mist swirls arnd em,
> n we'll smhw B preserved.

AN EARNEST CHESTNUT
FOR REMEMBRANCE DAY

In June 1918, a young poet called Eloise Robinson, touring the Front on behalf of the YMCA, was giving a poetry recital to an audience of American soldiers. Guy Davenport tells it: 'Reciting poetry! It is all but unimaginable that in that hell of terror, gangrene, mustard gas, sleeplessness, lice, and fatigue, there were moments when bone-weary soldiers, for the most part mere boys, would sit in a circle around a lady poet in an ankle-length khaki skirt and a Boy Scout hat, to hear poems'.

In the middle of one poem, Davenport tells us, her memory flagged. 'She apologised profusely, for the poem, as she explained, was immensely popular back home'. A hand went up, and a young sergeant offered to recite the poem. Here is what (in, as Davenport reminds us, 'the hideously ravaged orchards and strafed woods of the valley of the Ourcq, where the fields were cratered and strewn with coils of barbed wire, fields that reeked of cordite and carrion') the soldier recited:

I think that I shall never see
A poem lovely as a tree.

A tree whose hungry mouth is prest
Against the earth's sweet flowing breast;

A tree that looks at God all day,
And lifts her leafy arms to pray;

A tree that may in summer wear

A nest of robins in her hair;

Upon whose bosom snow has lain;
Who intimately lives with rain.

Poems are made by fools like me,
But only God can make a tree.

Eloise Robinson was surprised and impressed that he should know it. 'Well, ma'am', he told her. 'I guess I wrote it'.

Joyce Kilmer was killed by a German sniper less than two months later, only three months before the Armistice. His most famous poem had been published in Harriet Monroe's *Poetry* magazine in Chicago in 1913.

Eloise, for her part, continuing about her duties at the Front, wrote to Poetry that August: 'I wish I might tell you of my visit to the French front, and how for two nights I slept in a 'cave' with seven Frenchmen and had a hundred bombs dropped on me. Not directly on top, of course. The nearest hit just in front of the house. And for five days and nights after that I was taking chocolate to advance batteries, to men who can never leave their guns'.

Davenport mentions how Kilmer's 'Trees' is in fact a self-reflective poem, about poetry itself. These days that's a sort of workshop cliché, but — even though the poem rates itself as second to a tree — the fact nevertheless gives us a clue to something. Kilmer was regarded as the foremost Catholic poet of his day, and like a good Catholic he concludes as he must that however he may feel driven to create, his power as a creator can never equal that of God. This sentiment is in keeping with the sentiment of most people of his time, and is certainly in keeping with the sentiments of that far more famous Catholic poet, Gerard Manley Hopkins — and far more than (say) Ezra Pound, to whom he was connected through both contemporanaeity and the magazine itself. Pound may well have despised this poem for its utter lack of fearless modernity (though Davenport talks of its 'silvery, spare beauty' and 'inexplicable integrity'). But it had one important, unavoidable and perhaps even tautological quality (aside from the fact of its enormous popularity): it is a poem.

In his recent look at the satire of the recently-late poet Tom Disch, in the *Contemporary Poetry Review*, David Yezzi quotes at length from the following poem:

I think that I shall never read
A tree of any shape or breed —
For all its xylem and its phloem —
As fascinating as a poem.
Trees must make themselves and so
They tend to seem a little slow
To those accustomed to the pace
Of poems that speed through time and space
As fast as thought. We shouldn't blame
The trees, of course: we'd be the same
If we had roots instead of brains.
...
A sensibility refined
By reading many poems will be
More able to admire a tree
Than lumberjacks and nesting birds
Who lack a poet's way with words
And tend to look at any tree
In terms of its utility...
(from 'Poems')

According to Yezzi, this is 'Kilmer's earnest chestnut from the pages of *Poetry*... admirably cracked and roasted'. But I'm not so sure.

Kilmer may not have agreed with Disch's treatment, on the face of it; he had his religious beliefs to support, and his poetry was full of the inspirations and consolations of nature. Even his war poetry is about the nobility of suffering, with prayers and expressions of piety towards the dead, as in 'Prayer of a Soldier in France', where he describes in rhyme all the ways he is suffering, like Christ did, and concludes:

Lord, Thou didst suffer more for me
Than all the hosts of land and sea.

So let me render back again
This millionth of Thy gift. Amen.

I actually think this is rather wonderful. What exactly is the gift? By the same token one may wonder, when it came down to it, how consoling the lifestyle of a tree, with snow on its bosom and open to the rain, seemed to a soldier in a trench; by the time Kilmer came to recite it that day for Eloise Robinson, some of his fellow soldiers must have heard it as a faint, decadent message from a faraway world. But there must also be something wonderfully consoling about being, in some elemental way, like a tree.

Disch's poem, though, gets at something else, something important. Something that Kilmer — however conventional and pious — knew very well, and knew while he was writing Trees. It was the very reason why he would bother to write a poem about a thing like a tree in the first place — and the reason Eloise Robinson was reciting poems to soldiers. It was that while we are not trees, we have a solid core in us that makes us human, and that this core is expressed through poetry.

Let's take this day to remember not only the fallen of the Great War and other wars, but also their lives — however banal in their expression — and life itself. The fact that we use language as a human tool to engage with immovable, intractable nature — including our own nature — is more important to us as civilised human beings than almost anything else. It is, through being our nature, both an honour and also a responsibility. Lest we forget.

THE SEARCH FOR ELOISE ROBINSON

We all, it usually goes without saying, live in an eternally unfolding entity that we call 'the present'. We write in it, too, though the orthodoxy among writers is to say they are writing for 'posterity'. Most of our best friends, the ones we read and who made us want to write, are dead. They live in the past, though they lived in their own present, and they speak to us. We are their posterity.

Most of us, though, are not writing for the future: the future has room for only a very tiny number of us. We write with optimism, unable to see the future, and giving it our best shot. But, as I am always telling my students, every work of literature that even gets written is a miracle. Nothing *has* to exist, and nothing is foregone. The reasons why a poet sinks into obscurity, fails to deliver on early promise, or just gives up are manifold. The poetry magazines of a hundred years ago, which were greeted with exactly the rapture we expend on our own small victories, are strewn with the ones who didn't make it. When we read them we read not the past, but the present they were living in, where they remain.

Eloise Robinson, who appears by chance in a story about Joyce Kilmer on the Front in 1918, is one of these poets. She's just like us. She was touring on behalf of the YMCA, giving poetry recitals to the soldiers, when she had a small exchange with Kilmer, a few weeks before his death. It made a big impression on her — bigger than maybe she knew at the time.

We know this story because Eloise wrote a letter to Harriet Monroe, the editor of *Poetry* magazine, describing it. Kilmer's famous poem 'Trees' had appeared there, and they had also published poems by Eloise. 'I wish I might tell you of my visit to the French front', she wrote; 'how for two nights I slept in a "cave" with seven Frenchmen and had a hundred bombs dropped on me... The nearest hit just in front of the house. And for five days and nights after that I was taking chocolate to advance batteries, to men who can never leave their guns'.

Eloise wrote, and published some poems in both *Poetry* and *The Dial*, and at least one story, almost a hundred years ago. She obtained two very prestigious degrees, edited a well-received collection of the minor poems of Francis Beaumont, organised for her local poetry society, made writing connections, and then volunteered for the YMCA; met a fellow poet in the worst place on earth; and, shortly after, disappears from view.

She's been saved from oblivion partly by Guy Davenport, who must have heard the story he told as an anecdote, since it doesn't appear anywhere else. Ezra Pound — Kilmer's champion and Davenport's hero — may have heard the story from Harriet Monroe, his friend.

Looking for Eloise became a project, and with the help of copious research by friend and fellow poet John Clegg I have pieced together a bit about Eloise. Born Mary Eloise Robinson, in 1889 (or 1892), in Amelia, Ohio, near Cincinnati. She got her BA in 1910 from Mount Holyoke and her MA (the Beaumont book) from Wellesley, no less, in 1912.

By 1916 she is back in Ohio, 'one of the organisers' for the Ohio Valley Poetry Society. In early 1918 she sails to France as a YMCA canteen volunteer. Somewhere in there — maybe in 1917 — she went on a residential stay in a writers' colony, which is slightly memorialised by a letter, mentioning Eloise fondly, written by the wonderfully named Willard Wattles. She co-wrote a story with another fellow attendee, the playwright John Redhead Froome, Jr, which was published in 1918 in *Harper's Monthly*. We know where she was in 1918 — in Picardy. Poems were published — in *Poetry*, in *The Dial*, in *Scribner's*.

We even think we have a signed picture of her, found (I think) by another friend and poet, Mark Granier. It apparently was found in a box of photographs from the War, and the girl is the right age to be Eloise. She looks as fresh and merry as Joyce Kilmer looked in the picture of him taken in uniform, before he went off to the front (there is another, very different, picture of him taken a few years later, shortly before he died).

After this, Eloise disappears from view.

We thought about hypotheses. She could have got married and stopped writing — but why would she do that, when all her bios say her first collection is forthcoming? She could have been killed in the War — which as John said would have been 'astonishingly unlucky — much worse-fated than Joyce Kilmer himself', as she wasn't even fighting and the Swiss front, where she was headed on the night of her last letter, was so quiet.

We hoped she hadn't met an even worse fate, like that of Gladys Cromwell, another young YMCA volunteer — and also *Poetry* contributor — who must have known Eloise, as they were both reading to the troops in Picardy at the same time. Gladys and her sister Dorothea leapt hand in hand to their deaths, off the funnel of the ship that was taking them home from Europe.

Eloise's letters on the subject show none of the trauma that led Gladys and Dorothea to end their lives rather than return to a semblance of normality. On 5th August 1918, she wrote to Harriet Monroe:

One of the soldiers thereupon recited it—it was Sergeant Kilmer himself! This was only a few weeks before he was killed [...] I leave tonight for the Swiss border. And after that, Italy, and then the Polish-American front. It is all one mad scramble, but wonderful — simply wonderful. I cannot be too thankful I was able to come.

But there are two sides to this story. One of them is the search for Eloise herself — and she is misty. The other is her poetry, which was on the face of it a thriving concern. She was on friendly terms with the best poetry magazines in the country, had a growing band of contacts and a collection forthcoming, had been nominated twice for the Helen Haire Levinson prize, and was regularly publishing short stories too. In short, she was doing well.

Eloise Robinson was, in her very small way, a war poet. That she was deeply affected by her experience in Picardy we can see in the handful of poems that appear to be available. One is called 'War'. Another, a long one called 'Fatherland', won a *Poetry* magazine reader's choice prize for favourite poem of the year. And one is called 'The Trees'.

About three weeks before writing this essay I did one of my periodic searches and made a discovery. A poem — undated, with no provenance — on one of those free catch-all poety sites, by one Eloise Robinson Muchmore. A quick search showed what looks very much to be our Eloise, in the 1930 census, married and living in her native Cincinnati with her father James, her husband and two children (one called James). She doesn't drop out of sight until after the 1940 census — and these are the only two glimpses we get. The poem — so we know she *must* be *our* Eloise — is called 'The Sad Trees'. In 38 lines of abab-rhyming iambic pentameter, it tells of all the different kinds of trees and what they have suffered.

... They know the birch has given his white

Young body to be slain;
The golden larch, all day and night,
Upon his face has lain;
The olives cannot stand upright,
Their shoes let in the rain.
They think of how the willows have
Been beaten to their knees,
And scyamores that were so brave
Are scarred, grim ghosts of trees.
They gravely name the tamarack,
And whisper when they tell
Of aspens who brought nothing back
But bodies, out of hell.

All day the sad trees did not wink
Their shining leaves nor dance;
They were remembering, I think,
The tall young trees of France.

Somehow, in the perpencicularity of the trees, the economy of the
imagery, and the silence of the trees, this reminds me of another poem
about war: a passage in MacNeice, in *Autumn Journal*, describing the
ghosts of the conscience, of those who actually have been betrayed,
that are ignored by Londoners during the Munich crisis. It seems
clear that Eloise had a gift — for metaphor, for metrics, for image, for
timing — and a 'voice'.

In some ways the most interesting poem we've been able to
turn up is one that appeared in *The Dial*, called 'Blue Roses'. Of all
Eloise's poems, this one shows the real scope of her artistic ambition,
and the true cost of her experiences in Picardy. It also offers a sight
of her moving forward, and the reading she was doing. In a nutshell,
it shows 'Prufrock'.

The thick air beats in rhythms, measuring
One minute gone, one minute gone, one minute gone,
Of time that yet moves not, nor will,
Until its pulse is maddening
And I start up and shake the lethargy
Off of my shoulders, shrug
My weakness from me like a close, grey shawl,
Travel the floor, setting my feet mechanically
Between the round, blue roses on the rug...
There are blue roses, too, upon the wall
Thin, flat, blue roses...

The poem is drenched in the atmosphere of a hot day, stultifying and claustrophobic with flowers — but these weird, huge blue roses on the rug and on the wallpaper close in with menace that prefigures *The Yellow Wallpaper*, Charlotte Perkins Gilman's great feminist novel in which a wife is locked up for being 'hysterical'. There are no real flowers until near the end, and they are also claustrophobic: they almost even feel fake, a breed of Victorian survivals. The room is domestic but the discourse — the 'old comrade' chairs with their 'scars' — evokes the War.

The narrator, like Prufrock, goes round in circles on a moment where she is unable to take her own power in hand. There is no future, just the endless unspooling present in which the truth is impossible. The style also bears the tracks of Prufrock. Robinson was a Modernist. Her verse here is 'free', but with occasional tight rhymes, and the stops and starts and repetitions echo Eliot's then-recent poem. Her narrative is ambiguous, told in snatches of thought and perception: there is a death, a son never born. She stitches out of grief, clothes for the dead child? Through doing so, implicitly lies to her husband? Who doesn't, or didn't, want to be considered a coward, and signs (or signed) up?

"Hot fighting at the front. English retreat."
He looked at me
With the old grim, grey look
I thought my fears had conquered
And the room
Went suddenly most strange.
The lamplight made a sickly gloom
Over the rug's gay garden plot.
The table and the old comradely chairs
Whose every scar and spot
I knew, mocked me with change
Like words that rearrange
Themselves in hideous new meanings.
And I went upstairs
Where, in the chest, were laid
Wee, half-sewn garments never worn,
(He for whom they were made
Coming to us still-born.)
God! if the day were not so still.
Noon lies a dead weight in the room.

The poem is layered with almost too many layers of unhappiness to
be unpicked in the absence of any biographical detail. (As an aside,
Joyce Kilmer left a poet wife and four children at home when he
volunteered; they had lost a daughter to polio a year before.)

The poem is ripe with associations which, in the absence
of any real knowledge, we can have fun tweezing out. The rhymes
recall 'Prufrock'. The blue roses act on the narrator (and the reader)
like Gilman's yellow wallpaper; the whole scene is laden with this
nervy symbolism. It is quite possibly secondhand French Symbolism,
via Eliot, but who can say — we don't know what Eloise had been
reading. The poem also calls to mind, as John Clegg pointed out,
Robert Frost's poem, 'Home Burial'.

Almost more than anything, though, the nerves and uncontained agitation of the speaker seem to reach ahead into the future, to another great disappeared poet, also the child of Mallarmé and Baudelaire — Rosemary Tonks. The needle, the obsessive detail of the sewing, the loss, the heat, the inability to *say* it, the physical unrest — and possibly the loss of her art — is this the price Eloise paid for her War work? Did her writing, as in Gilman's novel, threaten the marital harmony? Did she disappear, like Tonks, because it was all just too close to the bone?

We can't, based on what we've found, know. The whole family, not just Eloise, disappears from the Cincinnati census after 1940. There is no obituary, either in or after 1918, or later. There is no trace that we've been able to find of another poem by Mrs Muchmore. Her few letters and the extant poems and stories are the only references to her in scholarly archives.

To say this story reads like a cautionary tale — there go you and I, fellow poets — is an understatement. There's no such thing as posterity. Eloise is our comrade and the proof that a few good credits and a forthcoming don't get you nowhere. Even John Donne languished unread for a good couple of centuries, until he was exhumed by the same TS Eliot. In this spirit, and in solidarity, Eloise is our sister and colleague. It's an honour now to read her poems and write about them.

> And when he answered I could hear
> My youth go by
> Turn from the room
> And pass out through the garden, down the walks
> Bordered by red begonia and pale stalks
> Of touch-me-nots and gilly flowers
> And white syringa bloom
> So into silence.

A HELL OF AN UNDERWRITER
THREE INSURANCE MEN WITH A DIFFERENCE

To whomever said there is no money in poetry, and to whomever answered that there is no poetry in money either, Wallace Stevens was quick to reply: yes, there *is* a kind of poetry in money. He knew about it, as he was an insurance man. He may even have seen actuarial calculations as a form of prosody — who knows.

Generally, as a truism, the arts likes to claim a moral high ground above the low-lying fog of grubby mercantilism; which is not to say that we are not all obsessed with getting a bit more money, especially these days, when about 800 people globally have all the cash that used to fund our schools and libraries.

Insurance, while a relatively new branch of commerce, is older than neoliberalism, and has its own points of connection with our little world of artistic concerns and what we like to call 'creativity'. Here are three unlikely leading lights of the life insurance buisness.

First, the 18th century Welsh moral philosopher Richard Price. Price was an important Dissenting thinker of his time and pretty much created the modern idea of life insurance. Dr Price had been involved with, and thinking hard about, the assurance and benevolent societies for decades when he presented a paper to the Royal Society in 1770 ('On the proper method of calculating the values of contingent reversions', according to the Richard Price Society's website). This helped what had been 'an unreliable service to commerce and individuals where 'bubbles' could and did bring financial ruin to many' become a service 'based on mathematically proven calculations'. Price's book

Observations on Reversionary Payments (1771) became a classic, setting the standard in actuarial work for the next hundred years.

Dr Price's work over his lifetime influenced several important areas of enlightenment thought: politics, ethics, and finance. This was on top of his work as an influential preacher at the dissenters' meeting house in Newington Green for decades, where he was visited by international thinkers and dignitaries including Thomas Paine and Benjamin Franklin. Dr Price was also a mentor to Mary Wollstonecraft, who had her school nearby, and was awarded an honourary doctorate from Yale University in the same year as George Washington. According to Martyn Hooper of the Richard Price Society, 'Dr Price's pamphlets outsold Tom Paine's *The Rights of Man* by 40 to one. He was a hugely influential figure throughout Britain and indeed the world and his contribution to the Enlightenment was immense'.

Richard Price is one of the three subjects of my poem, 'Richard Price'. The other two are Richard Price the Brooklyn-based crime novelist, and Richard Price the Informationist poet who works at the British Library. Neither of these other two has any connections — that I know of anyway — with the world of insurance.

In his day, Charles Ives, the American Modernist composer and 'Father of American music', was a very successful insurance executive. His 1912 booklet, *The Amount to Carry and How to Carry It*, was tremendously influential on the development of modern insurance practices, and the insurance company he co-founded and ran was the first ever to have a training school for insurance salesmen. Ives himself was the force behind the training offered.

Like Dr Price, Ives saw insurance as a social benefit, a way for people who lacked significant savings to be prepared in the event of calamity. His work came out of a social conscience. He also became very prosperous indeed — and it wasn't as a result of his music, which was neglected throughout his lifetime.

In fact, Ives conducted his insurance career and his period of musical creativity simultaneously, working full-time during the week and composing in the evenings and weekends. In this way he's a bit like the young TS Eliot, who wrecked his health working at the bank by day and writing his important essays and poetry before work. (The main difference here is the beautiful love story between Ives and his wife, whose name, amusingly enough, was Harmony.) In 1918 Ives had a major heart attack, and by 1930 he had retired from his business. He also, for the most part, stopped composing new work.

The rest of his life was devoted to getting his existing work performed; some of it he also published himself. There's an apocryphal story about the premiere of his Symphony No. 2 in 1951, in which he refuses to go to the performance at Carnegie Hall but instead listens in the kitchen on the maid's radio. The true version is a little less colourful. The 'Musicweb International' website tells us:

Leonard Bernstein and the New York Philharmonic Orchestra premiered the Second Symphony on February 22, 1951 in Carnegie Hall, New York City. The concert was also broadcast nationally. The story of Ives' reaction to the premiere is an interesting one. Ives refused to attend the concert, so his wife Harmony attended the concert at Carnegie Hall without him. In his biography of Ives, Jan Swafford relates Ives' reaction to the radio broadcast of the concert:

In legend, [Ives] heard it on the maid's radio and did a little dance of joy afterward. In reality he was dragged next door to the Ryders' to hear the broadcast and, unlike similar occasions, sat quietly through the whole thing. It was one of his soft pieces, as he called them; it was also perhaps the warmest audience reception of his whole life. As cheers broke out at the end everybody in the room looked his way. Ives got up, spat in the fireplace, and walked into the kitchen without a word. Nobody could figure out if he was too disgusted or too moved to talk. Likely it was the latter. (428-9).

The most famous insurance-executive poet of all, and the one I started with, is also the 'Father of American Modernism'. (They're all the Father of *Something*. Maybe actuaries are good at spotting a gap in the market.) Wallace Stevens worked his way up to be a Vice President of the Hartford Insurance Company, and kept his two lives nearly as separate as Charles Ives did. But it was harder for him, since his work was being published while he still worked at the company. He once barked at a young publishing employee who haplessly rang him at work: 'I told you never to call me here!' He also refused an event in his honour at the Wadsworth Athenaeum, a prestigious art museum in Hartford, saying, 'In Hartford I'm known as a businessman'.

Wallace Stevens used to walk to work along the same route my school bus followed, composing his poems as he went, and he'd apparently give a draft to his secretary to type up when he got in. This route now forms the Wallace Stevens Walk, an honour only afforded recently to the city's poetry prophet. (I rode this route for two years and paid so little attention that if I had had to find my own way home I would have starved to death.)

We know from his poems that Stevens had a secret inner life, a colourful one, and possibly dreams of another kind of life (or self). But his daily life was the picture of prosperous suburbanism, with a big house and a respectable family. Whatever was going on in there, he kept it under wraps. It came out in unlikely ways, one of which was a slightly nonconformist tendency in the workplace. He was a walker; he didn't drive. One day in, I think, the 1940s Stevens was going to Philadelphia for a meeting, and the company he was going to a meeting with offered to send a car to meet him at the train station. He refused; he would walk. They were flummoxed, but he insisted. They didn't know about his secret proclivities. When he did arrive, he walked into the meeting room, in the starchy insurance office, and put a large bag of fresh doughnuts on the table.

Like Ives, Stevens had a heart condition. He was told he would probably die in his fifties. Even so, he didn't publish his first book of poems until 1923, when he was 44 years old. *Harmonium* (not, so far as I know, titled after Mrs Ives) is possibly the most influential book of American poetry of the 20th century (a caveat I add only because of *Leaves of Grass* in the 19th). Of his nerves-of-steel decision to put off publication for so long (although he was publishing poems in magazines), he said: 'To publish a book of poems is a very serious matter'.

I once met a poet from Texas, William Wenthe, who read at the Poetry Café in Betterton Street, London. After the reading, he told me about a poem by the American poet Henry Taylor — who had once met a wedding guest with a story to tell:

Within a Stone's Throw of Greatness

Among the guests I talked to once
at a wedding in the late sixties--
back when the principals at such affairs
were my own friends, not my children's--
there was the father of the groom,
who turned out to be a vice-president
with the Hartford Insurance Company.
It had been almost thirteen years
since the death of Wallace Stevens,
but I put the question anyway.
'Yeah, yeah, I knew Wally.
I even know why you're asking.

I'm aware that he wrote poetry.
I never read any of it,
but I'll tell you this:
he was a hell of an underwriter'.

BECAUSE LONDON IS STILL A KALEIDOSCOPE

LONDON: A HISTORY IN VERSE, EDITED BY MARK FORD (HARVARD UNIVERSITY PRESS, 2012)

This — the moment of the 2012 Summer Olympics — is 'London's greatest moment'! So anyone riding on a bus in London last week was told by the recorded voice of our mayor, Boris Johnson — though he turned out to be talking about how best to avoid the crush on public transport.

By the same token, a rather over-excited official earlier this year appealed to Londoners, saying this Olympics was going to be the city's 'one chance to make a good impression'; and on the morning of the day of the opening ceremony, Big Ben rang outside its normal schedule for the first time since the funeral of the last King in 1952.

Anyone who knows London knows that its 'good impression' never depended on the Olympics. Since the beginning of what we can call English poetry — certainly since Chaucer started to write down the way millers and cooks and tavern-keepers really talked and acted — London, like no other city the world over, has told its own story in poetry, and the world has been enthralled. If literature is Britain's greatest gift to world culture, its drama and verse are a large part of why.

The English language has been nourished for two millennia by waves of invaders, beginning with the Romans; and waves of immigrants, from the Huguenots (see Gillian Allnutt's 'Museum,

19 Princelet Street, Spitalfields') to the Caribbeans we saw arriving in the Olympic ceremony (see James Berry's 'Beginning in a City, 1948'), and Asians from the Indian sub-continent (see Daljit Nagra's 'Yobbos!'). We have a huge vocabulary, teeming with nuance and connotative power. Our three greatest poets — Chaucer, Shakespeare, and Milton — have also created the largest bodies of neologisms. This process will never stop: Dizzee Rascal's performance in the Olympic Opening Ceremony, for example, demonstrated London's unique mixture of indigenous rhyming slang, Jamaican patois and urban American rap.

London's literary vitality depends on a powerful folk identity, the combined stories and personalities of its mongrel people — Napoleon's 'nation of shopkeepers', servant boys and fine ladies and rakes and priests — and the stories it tells about them. Canonical characters include Good Queen Bess, Will Shakespeare, Dr Johnson and his cat, Edward Lear and his cat, Oscar Wilde in Cadogan Square, and John Betjeman at St Pancras Station. And perhaps the most powerful presence of all: Anonymous.

Mark Ford, who has edited *London: A History in Verse*, knows all this. The book is as full of mayhem and colour as the city itself, and gives Anonymous his — and her — full due.

The tourists who flock here also know, for example, that Banksy and his fellow street artists are as essential to London's identity as the Queen. London plays tricks; poetry plays tricks.

This isn't the good impression the spokesperson had in mind last winter; they undoubtedly wanted something more like what a Scottish Anonymous wrote, in about 1500:

Thy famous Maire, with princely governaunce,
With swerd of justice the rulith prudently.
No Lord of Parys, Venyse, or Floraunce

In dignities or honoure goeth to hymn ye.
He is exampler, loode-ster, and guye;
Principal patrone and roose orygynalle,
Above all Maires as maister moost worthy:
London, thou art the flour of Cities all.

The book celebrates the whole city: what Jamie McKendrick describes
in 'The Occupations of Bridewell':

The loafers, the forgers, the feckless, the fickle,
The vagabond that will abide in no place,
The rioter that consumeth all…
Ruffians, cutpurses and dissolute women…

Jonathan Swift's 'Clever Tom Clinch, Going to be Hanged' puts on
a fine show as he proceeds down what is now our main shopping
thoroughfare, Oxford Street, 'to die in his calling':

His waistcoat, and stockings and breeches were white,
His cap had a new cherry ribbon to tie't.
The maids to the doors and the balconies ran,
And said 'Lack-a-day, he's a proper young man!'

Tom Clinch praises his arch-enemy, the infamous thief Jonathan
Wild, and tells the crowd his conscience is clear; 'he hung like a hero,
and never would flinch'.

Maybe three centuries before Swift witnessed this hanging,
another Anonymous had come to the city to seek justice — or at least
redress — for being robbed. He recorded his utter failure in a diatribe
to the heartless place called 'London Lickpenny'. Amidst the misery
of seeing his own hood on sale in a market full of 'stolne gere', he
describes the callousness of everyone in a position to help him:

In Westminster Hall I found one
Went in a longe gowne of ray.
I crowched, I kneled before them anon,
For Marys love, of helpe I gan them pray.
As he had be wrothe, he voided away
Bakward, his hand he gan me byd.
'I wot not what thou menest,' gan he say.
'Ley downe sylvar, or here thow may not spede.'

This story will feel familiar to anyone who's ever had their bike stolen, only to see it on sale in Brick Lane Market.

There will always be far more lore about London than it's possible to uncover in one place — or perhaps at all. Scratch a surface and another comes into view; scratch that... who can ever know it all? Ford's book packs in as much lore, as much fact and legend, as much gala occasion, as much glitter and cloud, gossip and prayer, sound and sight and smell as it's possible to imagine. The grand — the aristocratic, the heroic — take their places beside Hannah More's 'little wretches, trembling there/ with hunger and with cold', and WH Hudson's London Sparrow — 'blithe heart in a house so melancholy'.

London is full of presiding spirits, characters who still walk the city, flavouring it with their presence. Keats is among these; his wisps are everywhere; Hampstead Heath is rich with him. He is represented by three poems in this book. And he crops up as a character in two more, including John Stammers' wonderful 'John Keats Walks Home Following a Night Spent Reading Homer With Cowden Clarke' — an account of how Keats wrote 'On First Looking into Chapman's Homer':

God blind me, the star-struck heavens you contemplate

contemplate you in their turn, singular beacon
whose unrepeatable illumination inspires

...

Now at your desk, you lift your pen,
mutter something lost and begin to write.
Daylight finds you atrophied in ink, clouded in near-sleep.
By first post, you will be a masterpiece.

Not all of my personal presiding spirits are in this book. Since it is
limited specifically to poems about London, there is no Charles Lamb,
no Dickens, no Fanny Burney, no Mary Wollstonecraft. But Ford has
redressed the gender balance to a certain extent: the book includes an
array of women, starting with a ballad by the protestant heretic Anne
Askew — the only woman who has ever been both tortured in the
Tower and burned at the stake. The poem was written in Newgate
Prison in the last year of Henry VIII's reign. (In an interesting side
note, the churchman Thomas Fuller wrote of Askew a hundred years
later that 'she went to heaven in a chariot of fire' — a phrase that
memorably appears again in Blake's 'Jerusalem', which is not only
included in this book, but also serves as the title of an iconic British
film whose theme music was lampooned by Rowan Atkinson in the
Olympic Opening Ceremony.)

Between Lady Mary Wortley Montagu in the early 18th
century and more familiar Victorians, the book acknowledges
the late-18th century flowering of writing women. Mary 'Perdita'
Robinson, a notorious actress in Drury Lane, was a contemporary
of Mary Wollstonecraft and had attended a school run by Hannah
More. Anna Laetitia Barbauld was an influential woman of letters,
and lived within a mile of Wollstonecraft, in Stoke Newington.
Joanna Baillie, in Hampstead, was a friend of Barbauld. Charlotte
Mew and Frances Cornford, both writing in the early 20th century,
appear atmospherically. Isabella Whitney (the first 'professional'

woman poet, in the 16th century) is a gift. Her ten-page poem, 'The Manner of Her Will and What She Left to London and to all Those in It, at Her Departing,' is a glorious catalogue of all London can offer: its 'cunning surgeons', 'ruffians', 'quiet persons', 'handsome men', 'bookbinders by St Paul's'. With pragmatic generosity, the poet leaves 'widowers rich' 'to set the girls afloat', and 'wealthy widows' 'to help young gentlemen'.

This is a refreshing counterpoint to the pornographic romps of John Wilmot, Earl of Rochester, and the Anon who wrote 'In the Fields of Lincoln's Inn', with their stereotypical lusty wenches. In their London, women all love to 'swive' and with luck do so in public, with as many men at once as possible. (This gives the lie to Philip Larkin's assertion that sex was invented 'in 1963' – but that was in Liverpool, after all.)

As the book progresses into the 20th century, the vista changes. A more recognisable London emerges, a place of greyness, bad weather, boredom and buses, strangers on the Tube, and the isolation of the immigrant. Sections of 'The Waste Land' are exceptionally vivid in this context. Anyone wanting to understand last summer's riots – a year ago this week – could do worse than to start with Lynton Kwesi Johnson's horrifying 'Sonny's Lettah', a protest against the 'sus' (suspicion) laws that created a police culture where young black men get stopped frequently, for no reason:

Mama,
I really don't know how fi tell yu dis,
cause I did mek a salim promis
fi tek care a likkle Jim
an try mi bes fi look out fi him.

...

It woz di miggle a di rush howah
wen evrybady jus a hosel an a bosel
fi goh home fi dem evening showeah;
me an Jim stan-up
waitin pan a bus,
nat cauzin no fus,
wen all of a sudden
a police van pull-up...

Indeed, in this book, proximity to those in power is seen in all eras to
be best avoided at all levels of society. Sonny and Jim know this as
well as Chidiock Tichborne, whose 'Elegy' was written in the Tower
as he awaited execution, and Sir Thomas Wyatt, arrested for treason
on suspicion of having slept with the Queen, Anne Boleyn. While
in the Tower and not knowing his own fate, he could have watched
the vicious and protracted executions of the others (including her
brother) who had been arrested on the same charge — and even the
beheading of Anne herself. He wrote:

These bloody days have broken my heart,
My lust, my youth, did them depart,
And blind desire of estate.
Who hastes to climb seeks to revert.

Four hundred years later, another Londoner damaged in service to
the state — the First World War poet, Wilfred Own — wrote:

I am the ghost of Shadwell Stair.
Along the wharves by the water-house
And through the cavernous slaughterhouse,
I am the shadow that walks there.

The river, 'Sweet Thames', rolls on throughout this book, through the years and the centuries and events, and through Shadwell no less than Westminster. (There are, not just the famous one poem written from Westminster Bridge, but three.) Where Spenser walked 'along the shore of silver streaming Thames', seeing nymphs like brides, TS Eliot answers him 400 years later:

> The river bears no empty bottles, sandwich papers,
> Silk handkerchiefs, cardboard boxes, cigarette ends
> Or other testimony of summer nights. The nymphs are departed.

But the nymphs were there. Glyn Maxwell writes:

> violet and lime were the shades of the air that
> steamed or anchored over
> the slurping water, and this was the River Thames…

Tom Chivers, one of the youngest poets in the book and thoroughly London-bred, sees a modern river iin 'Big Skies over Docklands':

> From the train the water is not real,
> Does not move. The people, real enough.
>
> Mudflats the colour of petrol.

In 'The River Glideth of His Own Sweet Will', the poet – the late, much-missed, Irish-American poet Michael Donaghy, who migrated to London from the Bronx, via Chicago – lies in a hospital bed overlooking the river, and the river becomes Time itself. Time, of course, is an element this city is made of.

A large proportion of the book is given to 20th century poets – not just English – from Plath to Ashbery, from Thom Gunn to

Hugo Williams, from Ezra Pound to John Betjeman, and to young poets such as Chivers, Ahren Warner and Ben Borek, with his comic tour-de-force about a south London block of flats. Today's London is vividly present; it's laid out like a table of the jewels Isabella Whitney describes, or like a line of red buses along a bridge.

On this note, a couple of notes. The contemporary list is noticeably, overwhelmingly, led by Faber's (admittedly crucial) roster of poets. Admirably, Chivers, Warner and Borek are all published by indie presses. Though Chivers has blogged that he was never asked his permission to be represented in the book, I'm glad he is.

British poetry is undergoing a bit of a renaissance lately. There has been a plethora of exhilarating poetry in recent years, much of it engaged in various ways with London as a city, exploring her history, textures, presents and futures, her languages. Of course, every poem in this book deserves to be here. The trouble is that there are so many more.

I miss Anna Robinson's glottal-stopped voice in *The Finders of London*, for example, 'H', about the really poor who have always populated London — children and others who made their livings scavenging, including the so-called mudlarks along the river. Or something from Jon McCullough's *The Frost Fairs*, which begins to reclaim secret gay histories, some written in Polari (underground slang used by homosexuals and theatre people). Glyn Maxwell's verse radio play *The Sugar Mile* bears witness to the burning of the Tate and Lyle factory during the Blitz, and its human destruction. And dissident Chinese poet Yang Lian's poem 'Stoke Newington Scene', from his Bloodaxe collection *Lee Valley Poems* celebrates the importance of the 'local' to even the most international Londoner. I'd also have loved to see the Cockney skinhead poet Tim Wells — a bit of a legend on the London performance scene — make an appearance with his class-war dating poem 'Epsom'.

But these are quibbles. No one book can contain everything, and Ford offers a wonderful sampler of British poets, and of others who have washed up here and written what they found.

The titles of poems tantalise with evocative place-names, stacking up like gold medals: West London, East London, Bloomsbury, Ye Flags of Piccadilly, The Embankment, In Nunhead Cemetery, Sunday in Hampstead, In the Tube, Whitechapel, Fleet Street, Monmouth Street, Bunhill Fields, Parliament Hill Fields... Everyone's a winner, and there is an awful lot of London in here for anyone who wants to look.

THERE'S NO PLACE LIKE HOME
THE POETRY OF DOROTHY MOLLOY

Despite the proliferation of prizes and other opportunities for young poets, poetry remains one artform where age doesn't really matter. This is one of the main reasons why it will never be 'the new rock 'n' roll', and one reason why it is capable of being even better than rock 'n' roll. For example: despite being told (wrongly as it turned out) that he had a heart condition and might expect to die in his fifties, Wallace Stevens put off publishing a first collection until he was 44 – which would be like 54 nowadays. 'A book of poems is a very serious matter', he said. His first collection, *Harmonium*, turned out to be one of the most important poetry collections of the century.

In 2004, a slim volume called *Hare Soup* was published by Faber & Faber. Its author had hung on almost until 64 by the time her collection was accepted. She died of liver cancer only a week and a half before the book was released. It was received as a first and last collection in one. In the five years that followed, her husband, Andrew Carpenter, put out a second collection, *Gethsemene Day* (also with Faber) and a third, *Long-distance Swimmer*, this time in Ireland, with Salmon. Despite the absence of the poet to consolidate her presence in the poetry world, her reputation has been quietly established.

Anywhere you go in the poetry world you are likely to meet someone who, without talking about it much, loves and admires Dorothy Molloy. She was a superb technician. Robert Potts, a former editor of *Poetry Review*, wrote of a poem in *Gethsemene Day* that it was deliberately and appropriately noisy; and across the rest of the collection, it is impressively subtle and flexible. Sharp enjambments snap regular beats across line-breaks, while introducing a tug between smooth and rough metre by carefully placed internal rhyme. Echoes of nursery rhyme or comic verse vie with grave pentameter statements.

In her autobiography about being a young woman in the old Dublin poetry scene, Eavan Boland wrote about the need of a strong womanly voice, writing strongly about being a woman. Giles Foden, reviewing Molloy's *Hare Soup* in the *Guardian*, almost said something like this outright:

> If you want to read descriptions of genitalia in contemporary poetry you can find them in the work of Craig Raine, Paul Muldoon and Alan Jenkins. To the bark of these lusty stags may now be added the exciting new female voice of Dorothy Molloy, watching the prick of the hunting dog Kruger unsheath under the dinner table - 'a startle of red, pencil thin, sticks out of his fur'.

Dorothy Molloy was born in Ballina, County Mayo in 1942, and grew up in County Dublin. She studied languages at University College, Dublin and then lived for a time in Barcelona, working as a historical researcher, journalist, and painter; her work was exhibited in Spain, Ireland and the USA. Back in Ireland, she gained an MA in Medieval Spanish in 1979, and began to write poetry. With her husband she was a founder member of the Thornfield Poets workshop, a group that continues to meet in University College. I'm not sure there's even a recording of her reading her own work. This is a great shame, because hers is a voice it would be good to hear. A poet's voice can augment the work, and in her case, with the subtleties of tone - the dry wit, the heartfelt irony, the bitterness and aliveness, and her interesting pacing – it would be instructive to hear them read aloud by her.

It seems unlikely there will be many more poems from Molloy. In an exchange of emails shortly after I became the editor of Salt Publishing's now-defunct *Horizon Review*, her husband told me the only thing of any significance left unpublished is a 500-line poem called 'The Loneliness of Catherine the Great' – and if anyone reading this would like to publish that, I for one will thank you.

In an introduction to *Long-distance Swimmer*, Andrew Carpenter writes that 'more and more critics are paying attention to her work', and discusses a forthcoming book by Dr Luz Mar González Arias, 'which will set her work into a European as well as an Irish context'. Aibhe Darcy has written an article in *Oxford Reviews* (of which I've so far only had access to an abstract) that discusses Molloy firstly in the context of the American Gurlesque school, 'a camped up performance of femininity, lush with verbal music and kitsch imagery', and then in specific relation to Ireland, where it 'deploys the double vision of the Gurlesque to create spectacular, moving, and darkly funny evocations of the complexity of individuals' relationships to religion in this changing society'.

Despite this attention, in researching for this essay I was nonplussed (to say the least) to find that my own poor reviews make up so much of what comes up on Google. I leave them unchanged here – so they form not a considered overall view, but on-the-spot responses to her individual collections.

HARE SOUP, DOROTHY MOLLOY (FABER, 2004)

Dorothy Molloy's first (and, sadly, posthumous) collection is well-titled — a rich and aromatic mix of high poetry, religion, sex, essence of femaleness and cool observation.

The strangeness and delight of this broth are apparent from the first poem, 'Conversation Class', whose wonderful music and wit, and final telling image of 'the red flare of my skirt', set the tone for the collection:

> 'Encore une fois,' she zaps and taps her nails and sips
> her Perrier. My tongue is jammed, my teeth are in a
> brace. Her hands fly to her face. 'Mon Dieu,' she cries,
> 'Mon Dieu, qu'est-ce qu'on peut faire?'

The answer is: observe, describe, observe. And that she describes the inner life as intricately as the outer only makes her external observations more chilling, more powerful; sometimes what seems to be metaphorical suddenly reveals itself as possibly a literal experience, as in 'Burial': 'I made a little coffin / for my womb...'

> Electric fences hum in the forest of Fontainebleau,
> disturb the twig and branch, the hand and hoof, the bristle,
> and the silver-sickled tusk,

begins the dreamy 'A Walk in the Forest'. This is Perrault's forest, not the usual tourist one, as we know by line three. A couple more stanzas and the narrator is giving birth by herself in the night, surrounded by wolves and boars, and it is hard to believe it's not an enchanted cub she's giving birth to.

This is the first poem in the book to mention afterbirth. This reviewer would normally close a book of poetry on the appearance of this word, but wait! The icky too-earthiness is cut by the psychological complexity of this poem. In the other, 'Looking for Mother', she finds in her mother's wardrobe '...the scent // of oestrus, umbilicus, afterbirth, / eau-de-cologne...' The mother may be primordial, but she is also a woman who knows how to dress.

This book is full of sex. Molloy doesn't flinch from calling it as she sees it, through a prism of religion and family dynamics. Child abuse segues into bad adult sex and abusive relationships, and there are certainly knives, rapes and near-rapes. There is a poem that begins, 'We got there through the blinding fields of rape'. But throughout the collection her clear gaze and a deadpan survivalist humour (in the title poem: '...at the stroke of midi, we sit at the table, / Monsieur and Madame Vidal, the idiot / Didier and me. I force down / the pottage. The gun-dog salivas my knee') save us from the dangers of polemic and histrionics. There is real feeling here, based on hard experience, but there are also writerly detachment and intelligence at work, and absolutely no sentimentality.

Religion looms large and merges with the sexuality of the poems, underpinning everything, with blood the dominant motif: saints bleed, women bleed, stigmata are the result of living one's life. Everything's red — or 'scarlet and purple, vermilion, alizarin, / ruby, carmine and cerise.' A poem about a violent relationship (specifically, the man is violent in reaction to the woman's sexuality) is called 'First Blood'. In 'Plaint':

> The Virgin intercedes. She lets me stroke
> Le Saint Prépuce. The marble bleeds.

In 'The Infant of Prague', a poem suffused with both religious iconographic and sexual imagery:

[I] brush the pale

> of his cheek with my lips. Crimson embroideries
> seep through his clothes; there is blood on my hands.
> An ooze of vermilion
>
> darkens the flax of his curls. Water flows
> from the gash in his side. He is stiff as a statue,
> his feet are stone cold.

In 'Postulant' the atmosphere is thick:

> For morning Mass he chooses her
> to vest him in the chasuble
> and alb. He calls her
> 'Friend in Christ' and puts the host upon her tongue.
> She grips her beads
>
> and guards her eyes. He beckons her.

However, as well as a sacred element there is also a profane one: flowers are enlisted in large numbers, in almost every capacity except that of a normal everyday garden. In 'King's Paramour' they are used in a good old-fashioned witchy way ('...dittany, caper-spurge, marjoram, iris') for contraception and abortion; in 'I saved them in mid-winter' they are receptacles of knowledge; and in 'Burial' they officiate at the funeral like guardian angels.

In 'Postulant' the ingredients of the church incense take on the properties of a spell. In fact, the spells abound:

> ...if needs be, I provoke
> the red gush with mandrake and scammony,

colocynth, lavender, gentian and thyme.

The effect of all this is rather like a mediaeval tapestry.

Molloy's 'I' takes full responsibility for all her feelings, her reactions to events and for the significance things have to her. This is very grown-up poetry about the living of an intelligent, creative life.

This poetry is driven by a strong music, great big meaty mouthfuls of sound. 'Conversation Class' starts the collection with wonderful consonants: zuts, zaps, taps, sits, poof. The teacher 'cocks her ear and smoothes her coif'; 'I fiddle with my cuticles'. Awkward lengths, enjambment and caesurae, alliteration, internal rhyme and assonance make the lines seem to hurtle into one another, then stop short perfectly — the sense of timing is exquisite.

Sometimes the enjambments pall a little, especially the enjambed stanzas, and the solitary lines which often portentiously end poems. Many of Molloy's lines are halved iambic pentameters broken by caesurae. While this sometimes helps to set up an air of dislocation and urgency, they can also, read aloud, gradually revert to the traditional form. However, these are small quibbles with a very exciting and demanding first collection. Some small poems, like 'Eternity Ring' and 'Stalemate', are gems of perfection, and many others remain glowing in the mind like hot red coals. If not for Molloy's recent death, just before this book's publication, we would now be waiting with baited breath for her next. As it is, 'the Lady of Sorrows / glows in her niche,' with panache.

GETHSEMENE DAY, DOROTHY MOLLOY (FABER)

The Irish poet Dorothy Molloy's first collection, *Hare Soup*, was widely reviewed as being her both first and last book: aged 62, she had died of liver cancer just a few weeks before its publication in January 2003.

Now, however, we have a second collection, put together from the poems unpublished at the time of her death, many of them about the illness itself – notably the title poem, in which she awaits lab results (and presumably a prognosis). I'm not sure if all these poems were written after the poems in *Hare Soup*, or whether they were all new. I'm not sure it makes a difference. There are a few poems in the first collection that hint at dark times coming. But for Molloy, dark times were nothing new.

The physical manifestations of illness and death in the body seem a natural extension of her subject matter: almost her entire poetic vision seems to be channelled through the self-as-body, and particularly in the bodily interruptions of self: blood, sexuality, death: all obstacles to rational self-determination. Of course, in Molloy the flesh *is* made word – and the biblical reference here, in its inherently pessimistic reversal, is apt. In the course of this collection bits of the liver, uterine fibroids ('fruits of the womb'), her pubic hair, even her heart, are alien or lost:

> My heart lives in my
> chest. I know it's there.
> But now the rogue will often
> disappear, and leave me
> stranded in my scarecrow
> mind. It's so unkind.

Mavis the cat bites off her own tail in sexual frustration, being already 'short a few tits.' A dog is spayed in 'Curette' — the curette being the instrument that would have, kindly, left the dog intact. And the bits of the body that do remain cause endless grief and trouble:

Last night the itch was a witch
poking her switch in there.
The twitch of the sphincter no salt
or balm could repair.

(Of course, I love this one: the last person to rhyme on 'witch' so relentlessly was also called Dorothy.)
It's a cruel world, and death is in life. The villanelle 'Bones' begins:

I feel the bones that will lie in my grave;
They have for me a close familiarity;
They live inside me, snug in their enclave.

This constant death — peering inside the body to see what will fail first, like a macabre 'Incredible Journey' — combines with the sort of mystical magic that informed poems like 'The Infant of Prague' in the first collection. And indeed, many of these poems seem to bear out the effects of a specifically Irish Catholic upbringing on the rather strange, intense child Molloy must have been. In 'Death by Poisoning,' about the family dog, Bracken, ideas are mooted as to why the dog died — a rat; meat dropped by a crow — but it is the fairies who seem the most plausible:

The changeling's dead.
We left her in a sack

for fairies to reclaim,
bring our dog back.

She never came.

The child's perspective crops up here in poems about adult male sexuality, as in the first collection: 'I pretend he's a friendly old dog when he jumps in/ beside me and rests his white head on my knee./ But I find I can't slap him away when he opens his flippety-/ flap...'

This collection contains none of *Hare Soup*'s rather ecstatically sexual poems. In one poem 'Maria' is creepily and superstitiously desperate for another baby. In another, Molloy has a bath, where 'between my upper thighs, the bivalve seethes.'

Unavoidably, poems like this seem to owe a noxious debt to poets like Sharon Olds, and the women who went before her carving out a niche for poems about 'female experience.' Molloy presents the body as almost a barrier between herself and the world, as when people take her for a 'girl' and assume they know what that means; usually, of course, they're wrong; and this is all very well, as far as it goes, which is not, in my view, very far. It's hard to think of a male poet who writes about how misunderstood he is on account of having a beard, or hairy legs, or his brain in his willy. But Molloy's work — and I have no idea whether she would have called herself a feminist— strikes me as more interesting than that.

Presenting us with her very own fixated binocular-view of the misappropriation, Molloy becomes an almost Gothic character. Of the same generation as, say, Germaine Greer or Gloria Steinem — and two years older than Eavan Boland — she seems to share more territory with a Brontë.

It can't be easy now, and it *really* can't have been easy a few decades ago, to be a young woman poet in Ireland. Ireland has stronger cultural interests vested in poetry than many other countries do, and it is swarming with virile young men all wanting to make their mark. Dublin is no San Francisco: in the 'poets' pubs' the hard-drinking, womanising ghosts of Behan and Kavanagh still loom very large. Eavan Boland has written of the inability of a female poet to exist within some of the conventions of Irish poetry, especially to externalise the female identity of mythic 'Ireland' so as to occupy a male space in relation to it. Knowing nothing about Molloy as a person — and indeed I have never seen so much as a quote from, much less an interview with, either her or her husband — one could imagine that Molloy's fixation on the body, her expressed experience of sexual identity, and the fact that she published her first book at sixty, suggest the difficulties of the enterprise.

Any poem Molloy had written would have been a physical experience, in any case. Her very language is rooted in the body, and has a satisfying texture in the mouth. I have been puzzling over her particular approach to the poetic line, and the way it works with its lengths and stops, its enjambments and its caesurae, on her particular syncopation that picks up and drops metre almost foot-by-foot. It strikes me that Molloy's poems were conceived almost as little bodies. Like her, the poems have quite noticeable pletons. Because of this, Molloy can't 'throw out a line' as, say, fishermen do. Her lines stop, start, pick up speed and then have to carry on in the next one down, and are punctuated by a very distinctive use of brisk, flat vowels and clacking consonants. This sound is her own music, and it is the thing that makes these poems work despite their weaknesses of melodrama, sentimentality, and the sometimes lazy diction which leads to sloppy imagery like that in the second stanza of 'My heart lives in my chest':

The house inside my chest is
empty now — a vacant lot;
the weeds grow wild in there,
and still heart not come back.
Soon the foundations will be swept
away…

She annoys me with a slight histrionic edge, almost adolescent, as if she were the only person who had ever had a hard time. But then, Molloy never complains. She hardly ever even explains. She presents a clear view without interpretation, and her viewpoint is so sly, intelligent, intelligent and authentic that it commands respect. It is also not, for all that, a joyless or humourless view. For Molloy, the joy is in being herself, in seeing the world as she does, and in making these poems.

The book ends with a poem called 'Life Boat,' Molloy's own Noah's Ark. This story is intrinsic Molloy territory, in its darkness (which is both simple, to do with the fact of destruction, and psychological, dealing with questions about one's right to existence) and also in its Sunday-school message of redemption, hope, continuance. It can (of course; all poems can) be read as Molloy's creative manifesto. Busily she shores these fragments against her ruin. The poem begins, 'I made an ark out of my skull, an upturned hull…' and continues: '… till suddenly/ dark stirrings/ of my mind released the beasts within:// the onocentaur, oversexed, came rushing in; the manticora/ grinding/ all its teeth… For forty days or weeks or months or years, I waited/ for the waters/ to subside. The creatures in my cranium increased/ and multiplied…' till at the end: 'And lo, God's gifts/ lay scattered/ all about:' And I'm not going to tell you what the gifts were. You'll have to get the book.

LONG-DISTANCE SWIMMER, DOROTHY MOLLOY (SALMON)

The trouble with Dorothy Molloy's third collection, *Long-distance Swimmer*, is that odd things — starting with the title — take on shades of significance not intended by the author, but unavoidable due to the sad fact of her death six years ago. The other trouble is that it is apparently the last collection of her work we will have. Her first collection, *Hare Soup*, was published by Faber ten days after her death (aged sixty-one) from cancer. It was followed by *Gethsemene Day*, mainly made up of poems written during, and about, her illness. This third book, published not by Faber but by Salmon, is a slim volume, and the print is quite big. But, far from being the scrapheap of her work, it contains some of her most ambitious and exhilarating poems.

Molloy's characteristic sound is a sort of syncopation or counterpoint: lines, often metrical or nearly so, reeled off unevenly across well-placed line-breaks, often with short, three-or-four-syllable lines taking or throwing the punch. Layers of sound and meaning, internal and external rhymes and caesurae give texture and surprise to the poems. Her diction and syntax are simple — directly effective, as well as allowing space for the sonic effects to operate. Her tone is as uncompromising as her versification, and there is a lot of death in this book.

Numerous poems deal unflinchingly with her illness and treatment, and her impending (as it was then) death:

> I could arrange, like her, to wear a snow-white flannel gown,
> a violet posy at my throat, and in each hand a fresh-cut
> heliotrope...

But I must hear most needfully 'Last Lines' in its entirety

from Emily Brontë's pen. Then lower me into
eternity — the family plot. Engrave the words 'Called back'
on my small stone,

and on my death cert say my occupation was 'At home'...

('Thinking of Emily Dickinson')

There are two poems about a death by drowning: the same poem,
written twice in different ways. There is a harrowing one about
putting down the family cat. A vivid sequence about 'Federico' — 'a
phosphorescent child (since lightning left its / kiss upon his cheek)'
— portrays Lorca's childhood and sexual awakening with rich visual
detail. Its final stanza stuns us with death:

In August nineteen thirty-six, the death-squad came.
They trampled down the jasmine and the bright blooms...

But amid all the death, and deaths, there is life everywhere in this
book. There are poems about Spain, where Molloy lived for some
years, including a delightfully mock-serious poem about a toddler
trying to escape. She loves food; 'Forbidden Fruit', the poem about
Lorca, begins with a list of it: 'He loved dark chocolate, speckled
melons, quince'. And another Spanish poem, 'Christmas in the
Pyrenees', begins: 'Smells of hot chocolate and snow drift into the
room'. Even the toddler gets the gourmet treatment:

We went to the market, bought apricots, peaches,
black olives and anchovies,
almonds and quinces, *chorizos*, *serranos*,
manchegos and *churros*...

Molloy is a more fiery feminist than Ní Chuilleanáin, but just as unspokenly attentive to the realities of women's lives. In a surprise visit to the Middle Ages, 'The Dowager Queen's "Te Deum"', she gives us Emma of Normandy (arguably the most powerful woman in British history before Elizabeth I) on the eve of her legendary 'trial by fire' in 1044. According to legend, Emma — mother of Edward the Confessor, for whom she bore little love — walked over nine burning ploughshares to prove that she had not committed adultery with the Bishop of Winchester; she survived, and was thus proved innocent. It was the king who had banished her to Winchester in the first place.

> And I have sworn before the king, my son,
> who is a fool,
> that I have never slept with Bishop Alwyn;
> nor kissed
> the Lord's anointed one, except at Michaelmas
> his blessed ring...

Hers was a miracle survival, but the character of the haughty, ironic, angry, discerning voice of the Queen makes it seem only natural. It is a shame Molloy couldn't have achieved the same miracle. She is a sad loss — one of the most *alive* poets currently being published, in all ways but one.

MEN'S TROUBLES

NICE WEATHER, FREDERICK SEIDEL (FABER, 2013)
QUICK QUESTION, JOHN ASHBERY (CARCANET, 2013)
MORTALITY RATE, ANDREW ELLIOTT (CB EDITIONS, 2013)

Had things been different, and our nascent ideas about human psychological mechanisms come from a *female* Dr Freud instead of the one we got, we may well have spent the past hundred or so years asking: 'What do men want?'

What is this pathos, or even bathos, that afflicts them so? What is this truncated tragedy they live among? What is it they lack, and how do they compensate for it? What can we do about them?

If we *had* been asking this, three new poetry collections might well have helped to point us to answers about the male condition and its impulses.

Frederick Seidel, in particular, might be seen as a 'man's poet': he is often charged with misogyny (as well as other socially unpalatable attitudes) — to the extent that one magazine has said it gets hate mail whenever it publishes him. Seidel is rich, he loves Ducati motorbikes, luxurious food and travel, and he doesn't even do the poetry-reading circuit. There is a poem in his new book called 'Cunnilingus', and another about the death of Osama bin Laden that begins and ends with a paean to his girlfriend's bikini wax.

His new collection, from Faber in the UK and SG in the USA, bears the rather commitment-phobic title *Nice Weather* and opens straight up ('Night') into a vision of darkness and sexual violence:

The prostitute— whose name is Dawn —

Takes the man in her mouth and spits out blood.
Rosy-fingered Dawn.

But a stanza before we get here, we've been warned: 'Meanwhile, the customer is frightened, too.' When Seidel writes in this poem, 'The city sleeps with the lights on', he means just this, that everyone is frightened:

The insomniac wants it to be morning.
The quadruple amputee asks the night nurse what time it is.
The woman is asking for her mother,
But the mother is exhausted and asleep and long since dead.

In a poem called 'The State of New York', he writes,

You're a miracle in a whirlpool
In your blind date's vagina,
At your age. Nothin could be fina...

One thing that people who object to Seidel often cite is his ironic distance. The formal and technical he uses to achieve this distance – his cartoonish aaaaa rhyme schemes, his sentence fragments, his offhand expostulations – can grate on the nerves and skate perilously close to doggerel. But they are saved from doggerel by the fact that they call attention to – they provide surfaces for – the emotional depth of the poems. Seidel is, in fact, a poet who wears his heart on his sleeve, and he gives himself the same treatment he metes out to others.

In the poem quoted above, the poet almost immediately adds: 'Don't be a ghoul. Don't be a fool,/ You fool.' The frailty, fear, visceral physicality in the poems are always, at bottom, his.

His earlier style owed much to his teacher and mentor

Robert Lowell; over the years this has loosened up in an apparently huge debt to John Ashbery. But rather than merely exchanging a baroque, intellectual confessionalism for dandyish cartooning, the bright colour of this later style has brought him out, enables him to expand into a dazzling, capacious daredevil of a poet. He may well be *the* poet *de nos jours* of New York City; and this book brings the yellow cabs honking, people hurrying and shouting and getting laid, restaurants and eating and drinking, fireworks bursting over the Hudson and the ceaseless, nervy, reassuring hum of it all — the veneer of civilisation, and his deep attachment to it, while not being taken in — straight into your living room.

This new collection is that dreaded beast, the book about getting old. Seidel is in his seventies now. 'My old buddy, my body!/ What happened to drive us apart?' he asks in 'Midterm Election Results, 2010'. 'Think of our trips to Bologna…'

'The time is coming when it won't be maintenance./ The time is coming when it won't be minimal' ('Transport'). Elegies to dead friends, including the critic Frank Kermode, are as unsparing — 'Old age is not for sissies but death is just disgusting', he writes in 'One Last Kick for Dick' — as the poem 'London' is, about a woman so old and ill she can't even die, and the torn feelings of her grown children, which becomes a train of thought about what it would be like to try to go to Dignitas and have it not work.

The beginning of the poem about Updike made me laugh out loud though:

Updike is dead.
I remember his big nose at Harvard
When he was a kid.

Behind and beyond the panoply runs the spectacle of current affairs; several poems mention Obama, as well as other issues. As much as Frank O'Hara's, this poetry is a record of one man's life, in his time and place. Seidel possesses the great gift of being able to see; he doesn't filter what he sees to match what other people say *they* see.

In 'Lisbon':

> In sixteenth-century Portugal, there were thirty-two thousand African slaves.
> They came overseas in waves.
> They sailed over in their graves.
> It comes over me in waves.
> They died and went on living. At Cabo de São Vicente, the black Atlantic
> Spanks the gruesome cliff at the outer edge of Europe and gets sick,
> Throwing up white.
> ...
> I voted for Obama and I ask Obama if.
> Yes we can. I ask Pessoa.
> I ask Lisboa. Did they know about the Shoah?
> Yes we can.
> We can do anything known to man.

It's true there aren't many women in this book, besides girlfriends. But for any woman from our apocryphal mirror-time who wanted to know what goes on in men's heads, this would be a pretty damn thirsty, hungry and exciting place to start.

John Ashbery's new book has an even more non-commital title than Seidel's. *Quick Question* shows the poet, at 85, presuming not to know what's going on, but instead showing us the perplexities of the world. Perhaps, rather than the wisdom of age and the calm of the pipe and slippers, what Ashbery has to offer now is the experience of bafflement.

Ashbery, now the last surviving original member of the New York school poets, is famously considered the single most influential poet in modern American poetry. He was one of the post-Stonewall generation of openly gay poets (so there are no girlfriends' vaginas to be seen here) and has carried the flag for a sort of endlessly unrolling present moment ever since. Harold Bloom has called him 'our major poet since the death of Wallace Stevens in 1955' and indeed he 'resists the intelligence' — in Wallace Stevens' words — 'almost successfully'.

This collection, like his earlier 'later' work, has a cleanness, a sort of IKEA feeling, about it. Ashbery's characteristic pop culture references — as in say, his old sestina, 'Farm Implements and Rutabagas in a Landscape', which features Popeye — have given way to more general observations on how the world works, and how it feels to be in it while it does.

How it feels appears to be a combination of threatening, passively anxious, amused, and wryly detached from the main action. There is a vague sense of threat, mostly unnamed. Global warming makes a few appearances, as do mysterious unnamed 'they's; sleep is difficult to come by.

> So what if children don't dance, and burghers
> Recall their dignitas? It was your scruples
> Brought us here. I first read you that.
> The time to go home has been now.
> ('Palmy')

> A cloud blew up and like
> that: OK fun's fun but we got issues,
> so wait until tomorrow. At least that's
> what I heard...
> ('Etudes Second Series')

... Splurge and repent —
wasn't that the idea?
    'Quick Question')

Observations pepper these poems that feel like they're about the poems themselves, or about Ashbery's project. In 'Northeast building':

I tell myself I'm a minimalist,
not that it matters to the big guns
who train their sights on us...

In 'Elective Infinities', a traffic scene that could almost come from a Seidel poem exemplifies this; consider the weird off-kilterness of the word 'vacation' (which is, of course, American for 'holiday'):

At the intersection, a statue of a policeman
was directing traffic. It seemed like a vacation,
halloween or something. Process
was the only real thing that happened.

In fact, some of these poems appear almost to bear the influence of Seidel. 'Card of Thanks' opens with an uncharacteristic Seidelian rhyme:

Asked if he liked mutton, he turned away. No,
not here, today! And others might have it so.

But in these poems there is an emotional detachment that is more genuine in its surfaces than Seidel's ironies: Ashbery is more like a dispassionate observer of the world and its strange ways. You sense he himself is safe, wherever he is, though poem after poem uses the word 'we'.

His trademark style is suggestive. It's atmospheric. It's clever. It can be funny; and the juxtapositions are allusive. But when it strikes deep, it feels as if the depth comes from the reader's own associations. Ashbery is elsewhere, monitoring the ticker tape. The poems, as a friend says, can best be read 'as one would float down a stream', as a series of impressions quickly superceded by other impressions. It's an unspooling film of our nervous apprehension; or maybe life really is a dream.

> Blander scenes were always the ones farther away,
> but those leaves that curled in our hands,
> fig and nettle, survive in a notch of time
> clocks cannot undo, nor fortune despoliate.
> ('The Future of the Dance')

In once sense one might wish more peace for the poet in his mid-eighties; less the cacophony of voices you get in your head at 3am, and more of something substantial to show for it; but then, Ashbery has got something to show for it. Maybe we're the ones who have to worry.

> To be old only along the sea
> isn't a bad idea. One is turned
> into another kind of extremist.
> The weather gets to you. When it's wet
> you stay indoors. 'Plangent' is viable.
> One turns to one in tears, the sky shaking
> visibly.
> ('Absent Agenda')

Andrew Elliott doesn't pull his punches: his exhilarating third collection is titled *Mortality Rate*. It follows *The Creationists* published in 1989 and, after a long gap, the recent *Lung Soup*, both still available from Blackstaff Press in his native Northern Ireland. Elliott was one of a generation of Ulster poets including John Hughes, Damian Gorman, and Martin Mooney who (unlike older and younger groups of poets from the Province) have not built on early promise and recognition easily.

It's a whopper of a collection, weighing in at 150 pages (so there's clearly life in the old boy yet) of poems that start in one place and wind the reader along in their ever-deepening syntax until there's no way out, and then you're spat out at the bottom like the end of a funfair ride.

Not much is known about Andrew Elliott, except that he lives in East London, and appears to have spent time in both the US and Germany. There is no biographical note, and the publisher has had no luck finding out more. Asked to do a reading in a local bookshop, the poet replied, like Bartleby, 'I'd prefer not to.'

The poems give what might (or might not) be clues: that he lives in a tower block and sleeps in the hall because he can't afford curtains, for example; that he's fascinated by rubbish, loves watching people in the park, and likes Mark E Smith.

'I'm like the kind of man who...' This phrase, amounting to a refrain in the book, gives Elliott the air of an anonymous, everyman character — peculiarised by small foibles — or of a brave stance of self-definition; or perhaps of a sort of groping identity crisis, as in a Patrice Leconte film.

> In this, my second self-portrait in shades,
> I would like to begin by alluding
> To my first self-portrait in shades,

The unpublished 'Self-Portrait in Shades'
('Self-Portrait in Shades #2')

We know that Andrew Elliott is a film nerd; the book is full of movie poems, and indeed features a long sequence called 'Five Movie Pitches': Rom-Com, Thriller, Horror, Western, and Indie. And that some of his other poems are almost more like movies than these oblique 'pitches' are. 'Joy Ride' makes a mythic road movie out of poetry:

> I am driving in the Chevy Belair the Hofmann family rode in
> in Michael's 'Day of Reckoning', west across America.
> The wind has made much of my hair and, now tat the sun is setting,
> I indicate to overtake a pickup stacked with flat-pack quatrains.
>
> But as I pull away I note its right front tyre too rapidly unravel
> and as it swerves to keep control the pickup spills its way-
> ward load. I note all this in my rearview mirror just as later
> I will note the trailer park for which that load was, doubtless, bound…

Film references are everywhere, and in his adoption of the 20th century movie tropes the poet is also, of course, exploring the male gaze. Elliott, unlike Ashbery, is very interested in women: in their looks ('Librarian') and their legs ('A Man's Middle Leg is a Lady's Leg') and how it feels for them to live ('Tenement'). A lot of his women are *noir* women, as in 'Librarian', where the narrator addresses a librarian coming home to her flat and observed, as through a window, getting out of her work clothes — imploring her, whatever else, not to take off her glasses… It's hard to quote short passages from these poems because the sentence has always begun many lines above. The syntactical highwire act is always already in progress; the crane already swooping round for the tracking shot across the city.

To quote would be to fall.

As with both Seidel and Ashbery, but in a different way, Elliott's poems are full of soundbites. In 'Euro Trash' we see 'a refuse collector with one of those prong things' — maybe my favourite thing in the whole book. In 'Bin Man' we get 'her ego being boiled/ like an egg in its id'. This poem begins:

> I was rummaging in a bin in Berlin —
> It's a thing I did, I liked it —
> When I noticed, under everything, a briefcase...

This, in a single clear moment, begins the shaggy dog story. But these are shaggy dog stories with grit and wit and a sense of life's futile comedy:

> I was joking back there about the mesmerism. That's about it really.
> ('The Art of Discretion')

TO HULL AND BRAQUE: MARCHING TO THE DRUMBEATS

PANDORAMA, IAN DUHIG (PICADOR, 2011)

I an Duhig's fifth poetry collection couldn't have arrived at a better time (2010). With Pandora's box well and truly open, this book flies out among the little devils and reminds us that the ancient tradition of political poetry is thriving in contemporary England. Where Duhig's last book, *The Speed of Dark*, took medieval France and presented it as a Manichean mirror to the excesses of the Bush 'n' Blair Show, this one goes a little bigger — and darker. It's about who we are, and who we are is something desperate.

'Pandorama' is what the apprentice Bert White calls his panorama display in the early 20th century classic of working class life, *The Ragged Trousered Philanthropists*:

> The 'Pandorama' consisted of a stage-front made of painted cardboard and fixed on the front of a wooden box about three feet long by two feet six inches high, and about one foot deep from back to front. The 'Show' was a lot of pictures cut out of illustrated weekly papers and pasted together, end to end, so as to form a long strip or ribbon. Bert had coloured all the pictures with water-colours.

> Just behind the wings of the stage-front at each end of the box - was an upright roller, and the long strip of pictures was rolled up on this. The upper ends of the rollers came through the top of the box and had handles attached to them. When these handles were turned the pictures passed across the stage, unrolling from one roller and rolling on to the

other, and were illuminated by the light of three candles placed behind.

Without detailing every scene unrolled by Bert — with 'a suitable collection' played afterwards by the band, joined in at the chorus by his audience — one topical example may be illustrative:

> After a rather stormy passage we arrives safely at the beautiful city of Berlin, in Germany, just in time to see a procession of unemployed workmen being charged by the military police. This picture is hintitled 'Tariff Reform means Work for All'.

Duhig's book opens with a very modern prose-poem cut-out in 'goths': 'I love them. They bring a little antilife and uncolour to the Corn Exchange on city centre shopping days...'

But within only three poems of these creatures of contemporary decadence, he's giving us a good old-fashioned rabble-rousing in 'Charivari':

> Derived from chav, we call this charivari —
> rough music from us roughnecks plus a skit.
> Our instruments aren't made by Stradivari,
> they're anything that we can reach to hit.

And soon after that, he's playing provocateur to his target audience of poetry enthusiasts:

> You've heard that truth is beauty, beauty truth
> like one was Castor and the other Pollux —
> forgive the language of uncultured youth,
> but Cockney Keats was talking Hampstead bollocks.

Our Pandorama addresses repeatedly the links between identity and speech, song, and other sounds made by people working; and the mechanics of observation, of how we see. In the style of Bert's display, visions come, are described and sung, and are gone; echoes and hints and visions come back more shadowy and are replaced by new ones.

Like the panoramic diorama invoked by the title, this book is informed by a wide set of reference points. It ranges across the centuries, to and fro among the continents, and up and down the brow. It is demanding, and it's no use worrying about not getting allusions; Duhig makes liberal use of the knowledge he possesses, and doesn't try to second-guess which bits of it his readers might or might not share. The poems form a chain, linked by hints, as images and words appear again and again, chiming with and deepened by their appearances in other poems. It's like the march of civilisation, as if the subtext of the book was: 'Everything leads to something else' ('and something else again', as Paul Muldoon might add).

Duhig raids what Michael Donaghy called the 'posh shop' of Western civilisation, makes off with what he needs, and takes us on a rattling tour of his spoils. But while the shop may be posh, it was built by builders, and everything in it was made by people like 'Strata' Smith — 'a blacksmith's boy from that low stratum where/ language beats on your ears and means it'.

In this rich mix, an image of a Matisse cut-out begins a poem about boxing; the workers on the Great Wall of China echo the navvies on the Yorkshire railways; the Jesuit missionary Matteo Ricci (the very figure of a Renaissance man, later buried with great honour in a Buddhist temple) introduces a perspective-box into Ming dynasty China, and composes some ditties for the eunuchs (and in 'The Grassington Mandala', also, the religions jostle each other for space in the box). Leeds poet Martin Bell sits darkly in a pub next to a poem about the giants of Rombald's moor. Picasso and the White

Cube art gallery are not far away. Then again, a meteor 'is a poem…
this anti-philosopher's stone/ shattered the glass houses which
Aristotle built/ on Eudox's foundations, then Ptolemy gazed…'
(And, borrowing the conceit of Martin Bell's 'Leeds is Hell', this
same poem, 'A Summer's Fancy', begins: 'One day, soon after I'd
died, I returned to Hull,/ for my sins…')

Wallace Stevens is a presiding spirit, and strangely recurring
dark glasses in several poems evoke the eyes of his blackbird, while
the Saxon poets and the Kalevala also make appearances, and bring
Basil Bunting to mind as they come:

> The work of the Giants, the stonesmiths…
> … by files grimground…

> these many meadhalls men filled
> with loud cheerfulness…

Yorkshire — its giants, moors, bleakness, power and stony
outcroppings — is the ever-present, physical embodiment of
centuries of those who built it. The landscape becomes like another
kind of box.

Everywhere in this book are boxes: the perspective box
is rivalled by Cubism itself. There are memory theatres, Jeff Wall
lightboxes and a Joseph Cornell box, Chinese nested boxes; there's
a small town that only holds things bigger than itself, 'a Ptolemaic
nest': 'the Clock Tower/ at Shipley, a modernist white cube which
lords it over/ Market Square.' Even the earlier 'boxing' match comes
back to mind.

In 'A Room with a View', 'now I see civilisation through
new square eyes/ since buying a TV with two square metres of
screen'. A train carriage is 'this steel coffin with an Abbey view'. In
the same poem ('Jericho Shandy') a riff on walls recalls that Jeff Wall

lightbox (and 'cornell alarm chains' recall Joseph C's assemblages). A collection-wide attention to clocks brings us, via this train carriage, to a visit with Toussaint L'Ouverture in Jura.

And the drumbeat sounds in the distance. Drums are everywhere in this book, starting with the drums of the Charivari, like the Zulu drums in the old movies, rumbling like the movement of the earth underfoot. 'Braque's Drum' takes on the Colonialists head-on. A delighted piss-take of Sir Henry Newbolt's 'Drake's Drum' — itself based on a rather Arthurian legend that a snare drum Drake took with him when he circumnavigated the world can still be heard to beat in times of national crisis or momentous event — the poem reclaims meaning itself, for the people who need it. (As we write, it's tempting to wonder if Drake's — or Braque's — drum has been beating at all recently…)

Sir Henry's myth-making poem, to give the flavour, contains this stanza:

Drake he was a Devon man, an' ruled the Devon seas,
(Capten, art tha' sleepin' there below?)
Roving tho' his death fell, he went wi' heart at ease,
A' dreamin' arl the time o'' Plymouth Hoe.
'Take my drum to England, hang et by the shore,
Strike et when your powder's runnin' low;
If the Dons sight Devon, I'll quit the port o' Heaven,
An' drum them up the Channel as we drumm'd them long ago.

Where the Charivari drums are intended to beat the real 'truth' into the listener, 'Braque's Drum' begins with an epigraph from the artist (I translate): 'The drum, instrument of meditation. He who listens to the drum listens to silence.'

Georges Braque, 'e was an artist an' 'igh Cubist to the bone

(Sir 'enry Newbolt's spinnin' dahn below)
an' Stevens loved 'is Cubists an' 'e wasn't on 'is own,
  (an' spinnin' right beside 'im 's Picasso)
so multiple perspective's are 'is *Blackbird's* raison d'être
  (when such a view in art was comme il faut);
hence for this fractured eye on nature we're in Wally's debt
  (plus that poetry's another kind of dough).

(See earlier in the book, by the way, for a novel version of 'Thirteen Ways of Looking at a Blackbird': call it a Cubist call to arms for the workers of the world. 'Braque's Drum' is 'Wally's' third appearance in *Pandorama*.)

This poem embodies a truth we've forgotten about, in our craze for mass-produced, fame-based entertainment — where Simon Cowell, not Sir Francis Drake, is the hero we think can save us — which is this: that what we now call 'high art' used to be just as desirable to the masses — the proletariat — as to the upper classes. (When Picasso's 'Guernica' was shown at the Whitechapel Gallery in 1939, 2,000 people queued every day to see it. The admission was a pair of boots to be sent to the Spanish front, and there are stories of workers giving their own boots.) The Cubists literally taught us a new way to look at everything: the world split open, like Pandora's box.

They say poetry is the thing that gets lost in translation, that it can't be paraphrased. This book offers a minutely constructed instrument for examining the way we, that is *civilisation*, have tied ourselves up in knots. Its elements can be identified and partially listed, but the machine has to be experienced in motion. And we, no machines, are of the earth, as those stone giants keep reminding us; while the Charivari rings in our ears:

Because the beautiful can prove untrue,
you sometimes need to heed Tom, Dick and Harry.
We're here to drum that message into you,
and that's the meaning of the Charivari.

THESE FRAGMENTS WE HAVE SHORED AGAINST OUR RUIN

MYNE: NEW & SELECTED POEMS & PROSE 1976-2005, FRANCES PRESLEY (SHEARSMAN, 2006)
SELECTED POEMS, WS MERWIN (BLOODAXE, 2007)

As the poetry wars of the seventies begin to recede into memory, a new gap seems to be drawing attention to itself: the old 'divided by a common language' gap between American and UK poetry. I've been involved in a few conversations lately about how little reading is done 'across the pond'. In the US, British poetry is viewed as recondite, an acquired taste like PG Wodehouse; from over here, the American scene looks too huge to take in, and so fragmented, with its various schools and political factions, feuds and publications, and influences that don't seem to apply here in the UK and that we can't make sense of it. Much poetry from either country is simply hard to get hold of in the other.

Correspondingly, if it can be said that there are (loosely) two branches of Modernism, where the Pound-Eliot branch might be said to be the 'English' side of the tree — with its density of allusion and layering of meaning — the other, the Pound-Williams branch, the 'American' cousin, casts meaning wide open and prefers good old Yankee straight talk to decadent European obfuscation.

Two new books act as exemplars of these strands, and show how closely the blood line runs between the two sides of the family. WS Merwin's *Selected Poems* brings a major American poet into print in the UK for the first time in 35 years, and Frances Presley's *Myne: New*

& Selected Poems & Prose 1976-2005 acts as a mid-career retrospective (with major new work) of an English poet with a very different approach to many of the same concerns Merwin addresses.

Both these poets are politically and spiritually oriented in relation to their work. Merwin was an anti-Vietnam poet in the 1960s, incorporates the worldview of Buddhism into his poetry, and is known for his environmentally-aware nature poetry. Presley's overtly feminist poetry is also full of myth, which she handles in very different ways from Merwin. Her poetry is rooted in — indeed, born out of — the landscape of Somerset; Merwin lives in Hawaii, where he devotes his non-poetry time to environmental activity. Both poets are overwhelmingly concerned with the juncture between words and landscape, words and nature, words as the medium of human experience and meaning.

Frances Presley's *Myne* starts with two new sequences, *Stone Settings* and *Myne*. These sequences take their shapes on the page from the landscapes they have grown out of (this doesn't seem a whimsical way of putting it). Presley wrote the poems on site, many on specified dates; in an interview she says that during the writing of one poem she was 'literally dripping rain water onto the page!'

Stone Settings is a series of meditations on the unusual formation of Neolithic stones on Exmoor and is set 'in roughly geometric formations or apparently randomly'. It is written with reference to archaeological sources as well as the landscape: an exploration of ancientness itself, the layers of the unknown, parsed through what we can see and what we can know. The poem 'Hazel Eardley-Wilmot' (named after an archaeologist of the region) begins with a description that could apply to Eardley-Wilmot, or Presley, or indeed the reader of the poem:

The Author

acquainted with

      vagaries of language

does not

claim to be

more than

a serious amateur

      archaeologist

This passage names the search, the attempt to excavate meaning from the landscape itself — as if each word were a stone laid by an ancestor we can barely imagine, but who was speaking, somehow, directly to us, as through a string stretched between two tin cans — which distinguishes both of these new sequences.

Even as our ancestor said it, s/he may not have known what it is s/he was saying. Three poems on, in the prose piece 'Brer':

'...He said that it can't be Euclidian geometry except by accident and without understanding the angles. Even the Egyptians . . . . and this was so much later and so much less ... Only those without memories roam the moor at night. An oblique equilateral parallelogram. How can we follow these parallel lives? ... *From here to Withypool Circle is a precisely straight line of six and a half miles.* But they would not have had lines of sight, he says. They could not have known and there will always be a straight line between two points.'

The excavation is also, of course, of the Western poetic canon, which is the reliquary of our culture. Coleridge is never very far away in this sequence; he pops up in the numerous mentions of the Somerset town of Porlock, which acts as a mnemonic or talisman for the very act of forgetting (the 'person from Porlock' at the door having been the apocryphal cause of Coleridge forgetting the rest of 'Kubla Khan', which had apparently come to him whole in his sleep). In *Triscombe Stone (4)* he is overtly mentioned, taking on the quality of a point on the aforementioned straight line: 'Smaller than I remember, not even shoulder-high. People were shorter in Coleridge's bed, and we were closer together…'

Also dotted along the string, but unseen, are the women of Somerset, the old goddesses and witches. Equally, Presley seeks to excavate them within their landscape:

'three   and   thrice

      The   Werd

Systrys

hand   in   hand

                    chanting'

All language reduces — as a sauce or magic potion reduces — to essence, as the Werd, or weird, or word, Systrys very well know.

Another poem examines the attempts of another female archaeologist, Dina Portway Dobson, to know the landscape, evoking the impossibility of saving anything from the joint floods of time and space:

'Everything cannot be — included —

Attempt to summarize

to the end of 1930

To theorize significance

is another

difficult matter'

This is underscored by a quotation from Francis Bacon, embedded in
the poem and given resonance by the stones it seems to echo off:

*'Out of monuments, names, words, proverbs, traditions, private records and
evidences, fragments of stories, passages of books that concern not story*

industrious persons

do save and recover

from the deluge of time'

The series *Myne*, which gives the book its title, was written in 2003-4
in and around Minehead, Somerset, and the poems are dated —
emphasising the specificity of the given landscape at a particular
time, through the particular lens of the poet.

These poems chip away at the nonessential in the words they
are made of, becoming prisms of association and fractal intensity.
The words — our units of understanding — literally come apart,
breaking into their constituent elements so that the various pieces of
their meanings emerge into view, as in 'in St Michael's':

lip slide
these women had not
exerted themselves
had not
broken any rings
corseleted
corsle
cors'

Presley defines her poetic project partly in terms of visual art; much of her work, including this sequence, has been produced in collaboration with visual artists. This is consistent with her declared interest in Pound's placement of the image at the centre of the poem, and she herself uses the image, as she says, as a release from the lyric 'I' with its attendant hierarchies.

In the first poem, 'March// On North Hill' (for Tilla Brading):

lower buds
thinking without

Tilla, the tides
the tides
are always too early
or too late
to swallow
words'...

In 'April// from Greenaleigh to Porlock Bay', the image 'these black shards/ scattered on the field/ where sheep and walkers go// piecing together/ piecework' begins a piecing of soundwork that seems to spiral in on its sibilant sounds, though salt marshes:

walking back past lambs
he was talking ahead of me
about the Sybilline
lore and the ambiguity of
Sybilline law

These poems operate for me in much the same way as a piece of installation art, or the colour-field paintings of a Barnett Newman, say: reducing what is seen to its most essential particulars and removing all contextual meaning, which might cause the viewer — or reader — to assume things that are not in the text. They set up a pure aesthetic which operates by way of *reverb-* (note that word root) *-eration*.

The book also contains Presley's entire previous collection, the hybrid *Somerset Letters* — which looks at local life in vivid prose segments interspersed with poetry — and selections from her first three books.

Much of this deals overtly with feminist themes and the lives of women, and is often — unlike the new work — rich in anecdote and humour, as in 'Sari':

'She wrapped it round me making
the three folds or
if you want it tighter make it five
"Tighter is better for work"
Because the chiffon is all borders
You can refind the pattern
However you fold it...

In the living room
the men are solving
the new maths'

Other poems are about the life of the artist, politics and philosophy, as well as Somerset: Coleridge again, and Highgate Cemetery, and letters addressed to friends.

Presley, who was born in 1952, is very much of the English branch of the Modernist family. Even aside from the overt subject matter of the ancient English countryside, her poetry is almost misty as a legend, casting colour like a raindrop on an old oak. Her engagement with the challenges of form and language — that is, engagement as battle, against the danger of getting too comfortable with the hierarchy inherent in either system — grows directly out of her early reading of Pound's famous essay, 'A Few Don'ts', his call to 'make it new', and, as mentioned above, in his radical restructuring of the poetic image. She has coupled this with a radical spirit which recalls the old English spirit of rebellion. It's good to have her work so concisely available.

WS Merwin has said in an interview that, after years of searching for what was truly an 'American' poetry, he has stopped caring whether what he wrote was American, or came out of an American 'tradition', and settled down simply to write good poetry. This tactic seems to have worked, because his poetry emerges now as if directly from the landscape he inhabits — a cultural landscape, first of all, which seeks to clarify and explain itself, which values simplicity of act, expression and moral vision even while it prizes above all the multiplicity of the riches of the world, both physical and spiritual. This is the culture that produced Whitman, Emerson, Dickinson and WC Williams.

The physical landscape of America has always stood in the foreground of American literature. It is so huge, so multifarious, and the demands it makes on those who live in it are so straightforward, and sometimes extreme, that it seems to ask for those qualities in its literature. Over five decades WS Merwin has produced a body of work that incorporates his engagement with classical and canonical literature, spiritual concerns and the native lore of North America, in language as clear and refreshing as a river filled with leaping trout. His landscape is very much peopled: by people, by shapeshifters and gods, and by animals who are equally vivid in profusion or near-extinction.

Merwin, a scholar of the Romance languages, is a distinguished translator of work as diverse as *El Cid* and contemporary South American poetry. His introduction to his own translation of Dante gives a vivid account of Dante's world, his poetics, and his effect on Merwin: 'Since adolescence I have felt what I can only describe as reverence for him... of course, because of his poetry, and because of some authority of the imagination in the poetry, some wisdom quite distinct from doctrine, though his creed and his reason directed its form. I am as remote from his theological convictions, probably, as he was from the religion of Virgil, but the respect and awed affection he expresses for his guide sound familiar to me'.

Classical myth, accordingly, looms large (early poems are titled 'Leviathan', 'Odysseus', 'Learning a Dead Language'). There is a version of Catullus XI, in Sapphics; and the title poem of his second collection, 'The Drunk in the Furnace', features Orpheus as an old drunk living in a clapped-out iron furnace in a gully:

'...But the stuff keeps him musical:
Hammer-and-anviling with poker and bottle
To his jugged bellowings, till the last bellowing clang
As he collapses onto the rioting
Springs of a litter of car seats ranged on the grates,
    To sleep like an iron pig.'

From this sturdily canon-saturated beginning Merwin became a prominent Buddhist, 'anti-imperialist, pacifist and environmentalist'; after establishing his reputation with a book of formal poetry (of which only one example is represented in this selection) he began to move 'beyond... traditional verse' into the 'revolutionary open forms' (quotes from the back of the book) which are his trademark. Merwin's characteristic late style avoids punctuation and linear narrative — though stories are certainly told, and more plainly than in Presley, for example. This has the effect of thrusting the reader right into the words themselves, undiluted by all the hesitations and qualifications of the comma, semi-colon and full stop.

'The Judgement of Paris' (1970), finds him still exploring classical themes in this much more open style. Tellingly dedicated to Anthony Hecht, it describes the allure of each of the three beauties as a trap, of which the greatest trap of all is Helen's humanity.

> 'here was his mind
> filled utterly with one girl gathering
> yellow flowers
> and no one like her
> the words
> made everything seem present
> almost present
> present
> they said to him *Take*
> *her*
> *you will lose her anyway*'

He finds himself holding out a golden apple, inscribed to — in an echo of Snow White — '*the fairest*':

> 'then a mason working above the gates of Troy

in the sunlight thought he felt the stone
shiver

in the quiver on Paris' back the head
of the arrow for Achilles' heel
smiled in its sleep

and Helen stepped from the palace to gather
as she would do every day in that season
from the grove the yellow ray flowers tall
as herself

whose roots are said to dispel pain'

This passage hints at several theme of Merwin's mature work, including loss — or more accurately the folly of trying to hold on to things; the power of words to shape experience; and the nature of being human.

The humanity we carry in Merwin, like that in Frances Presley's stones, is invested with a meaning we must decipher. In his poem 'Hearing the Names of the Valleys' this task, our life's work, is futile, because the meaning transcends the words by which we know it:

'I have lived without knowing
the names for the water
from one rock
and the water from another
and behind the names that I do not have
the colour of the water flows all day and all night
the old man tells me the name for it
and as he tells me I forget it'

'For a Coming Extinction' is addressed to the grey whale, in the form of messages from humanity to the Maker of the whale:

> 'Tell him
> That we who follow you' (to 'The End/ That great god') 'invented forgiveness
> And forgive nothing
>
> ...The sea cows the Great Auks the gorillas
> The irreplaceable hosts ranged countless
> And foreordaining as stars
> Our sacrifices
> Join your word to theirs
> Tell him
> That it is we who are important'

I'm not equipped to criticise the quality of Merwin's Buddhism; what I can detect of Buddhist belief sits so lightly in his poetry that had I not known his identification with it I might not have spotted it as a category. It merely comes across as engaging wisdom. The next poem in the book, exercising this trait, takes a more forgiving view of humanity, as simply a type of creature with its own foibles, while at the same time nodding to our arrogance (and at WCW):

'As the stars hide in the light before daybreak
Reed warblers hunt along the narrow stream
Trout rise to their shadows...

> ...I dreamed that the heavens were eating the earth
> Waking it is not so
> Not the heavens
> I am not ashamed of the wren's murders
> Nor the badger's dinners

On which all worldly good depends
If I were not human I would not be ashamed of anything'

In 'Fox Sleep', the poem that gives his 1996 collection *The Vixen* (with its uncharacteristically long lines) its title, the landscape breathes through its artefacts of human life, a man takes the form of a fox (in a passage that reads strongly like a native American Jesus myth via Ted Hughes), and inanimate things are saturated with significance as if it were in the dew drying on the 'few relics of the life before… / after whatever they had been made for was over'. The poem's second section begins:

'What I thought I had left I kept finding again
       but when I went looking for what I thought I remembered
   as anyone could have foretold it was not there',

and the poem finishes with Merwin burying the dead vixen — the vessel of meaning, or poetry — 'in the morning of the clear autumn that she had left':

'There are the yellow beads of the stonecrops and the twisted flags
   of dried irises knuckled into the hollows
   of moss and the rubbly limestone on the waves of the low wall
   the ivy has climbed along them where the weasel ran…
   …and there beyond the valley above the rim of the wall
   the line of mountains I recognise like a line of writing
   that has come back when I thought it was forgotten'

WS Merwin is in his eighties now, and the few new poems at the end of the book all — in good Buddhist style — seem to be about leave-taking (and betray no fear of the lyric 'I'!). They are: 'By Dark' ('When it is time I follow the black dog'), 'Good Night' ('sleep softly my old love/ without end in the dark'); 'At the Bend' 'I wait for you my promised day/ my time again my homecoming'); 'Just This' ('how did this haste begin this little time'). The final poem in the book, 'The Nomad Flute', ends:

'I will listen until the flute stops
and the light is old again'

It feels necessary to say something about the extent of this selection. It is wonderful to have this book in print in the UK, but readers who want more will definitely want more. Merwin's oeuvre is vast, taking up nearly a foot (for example) in the Poetry Library in London (I checked). The selection doesn't contain his translations, and from his first book (not characteristic of his work as a whole, but interesting, and highly praised by Auden) there is only one poem. Many thanks are due to Bloodaxe for publishing this selection, and it is to be hoped that there will be more.

GIFTS OF EARTH

LETTERS OF TED HUGHES, SELECTED AND EDITED BY CHRISTOPHER REID (FABER, 2007)

Letters, though most people aren't around to see them published, are a make-or-break part of a modern poet's career, crystallising him or her in our minds and solidifying the mythos of the poet. That this seems not to be true of, say, novelists is an indication of the position of mystery poets still hold in the cultural imagination. (We see this at work in, say, Don Paterson's TS Eliot Prize lecture, in which he presented poetry as a 'dark art', suggesting that its practitioners have arcane or even shamanic powers — a view Ted Hughes might well be happy to share).

We shouldn't take this as a sign of an unhealthy obsession with the poet as an artefact of his own life — although Hughes certainly had something to say in his letters about 'fashionable' biographies. Literary letters have had golden ages as a recognised form of discourse, as a source of the wisdom of those whom we trust to be wise — at least wise enough to impart some insight to us, the uninitiated. Precisely because they are not the poems, because they are not constructed and mediated in the same way as the art, the letters become a platform for another, unique kind of writing. They are gems — like poems, but the poems are one thing; the letters are another.

It turns out that Ted Hughes — already more than famous enough for both his poetry and the more conspicuous disasters of his life — wrote wonderful letters. Christopher Reid uses the word 'generous' in his introduction, and generous these letters are. They are so genuinely interesting that I wished he hadn't said that, so that I could have had the pure surprise of the magnitude of that discovery. All these fifty years' worth of letters are long, discursive, honest. They are about daily events and news and thoughts and ideas and business; they are personal, in a way that few people even have the gift to be. In them, it seems that Hughes writes much as he must have talked: directly and forcefully, with complete engagement. At times they are almost unbearable to read, and not just at the times everyone would expect. Some of them feel like a gift, given — though addressed to someone else — direct to you, the reader.

It is impossible, reading this book, to accuse Hughes of any kind of cynicism, of writing with an eye to eventual publication. Although he must have been aware of the likelihood of publication, the later letters do not differ in personality or type from the earliest he wrote. They are an impressive record of an intense, engaged personality over nearly its whole lifetime and as such, whether he planned their eventual appearance or not, they are remarkable.

The most impressive thing about them is, of course, Hughes himself. He emerges from the mists of his childhood — still almost within it, really, on National Service — full of passions and energy and intellectual force. He had plans, always plans. For quite some considerable period in his twenties he was going to emigrate to Australia: 'there is a girl here that I shall take with me if I still feel like it, and probably marry her before I go,' he writes to his parents in 1954, of someone he never married. Then he wanted his brother Gerald, who did emigrate, to come back and run a mink farm with him, and he demonstrated the research. But writing to his parents about the Australia plan, he says: 'I have written to Australia House, and they tell me mink are definitely 'out'.' It was cheaper in Canada, apparently. In 1955 he was going to buy a house and let it to students and nurses at £3 a room: 'If we could get a line of houses running,' he writes, 'there'd be no need to buy aircraft parts.' In early 1956 he wrote to Olwyn: 'I discovered the other day that one can live in Hungary even more cheaply than in Spain...'

His letters were full of financial calculations and all sorts of money-making schemes. He must have been very canny, as he managed to run two households in what sounds like some degree of expansiveness, with help in the garden and so on, all on the 'sale' (as he puts it) of poems and associated activities. In the mid-sixties, though, he cites the rent on a huge Irish farmhouse as being £2 a week; this puts his $4,800 stipend as 'honorary member of the Philosophischen Fakultät' at the University of Vienna, cited in the same letter to Sylvia's mother, in some perspective. (All he had to do to earn this money was 'exercise his poetic talent.')

Hughes' determination to write, to make the space to write, determined all his decisions, from youth onwards. His faith in what he knew he had to do never wavered. At Cambridge he wrote to Gerald: 'I go to bed about 11, and get up at 2-30 in the morning. Then I work, and sing, and spring about amusing myself... until about 7, then I go to bed until 9-30. By this means I get two first sleeps and feel fresh as a flower... This is like leading two lives.'

His sense of poetry, and of his own judgement in it, was seemingly born whole: to his sister Olwyn in 1952, from Cambridge, he wrote: 'Swift is the only stylist.' To Sylvia Plath, not long after they met, and presaging his lifelong gift for teaching: 'How much reading do you do a day? Do you get through the books? Are you browsing with appalled boredom through the English book of Verse — Oxford of English I mean? ... The minor Elizabethans are interesting, and all alike. Try and see what their favourite gimmicks are, how they use metaphors, their rhythms, — the dramatic and yet colloquial tone of voice, as different from the late 17th and 18th whose tone of voice is personal and dramatic but flat literary. Note the artificial complexity of Donne's followers. A difficult period is mid-18th century onwards, when glorification of gardens turns to glorification of wild Nature as seen from over a silken cravatte.' 'Browse a lot,' he wrote to her, 'but don't let browsing obscure and dissipate your main line of singleminded reading.'

Hughes was always, in his letters at least, so confident of his own abilities, his own 'main line,' that it seems superfluous even to call it confidence. This isn't egotism: it is a clear, unalterable sense of one's self; he might like it to be called his Destiny. But about his work he was never vain, questioning it, appraising it, criticising it. He knew how he wanted it to be and worked to make it that way. You picture him writing with his sleeves rolled up.

Hughes traces a straight mystical line back through Blake, Milton, Shakespeare to the earliest myths. His interest in astrology — and what we would now call 'Mind Body Spirit' — is apparent in these early letters, as in this to Olwyn in 1955: 'My host — a monstrously built Pisces...' Or to Gerald: 'You could become internationally famous — you're a Gemini, and according to antique authority have a literary talent...' Many of his letters contain sketches of the recipients' astrological charts or descriptions of other people's, and he is later seen begging, for example, Faber to publish his books on auspicious dates.

He and Sylvia famously dabbled with Ouija boards — in one letter he describes a spirit who kept swearing and refused to answer questions, saying it was tired. They asked a more co-operative one to recite its favourite line of Shakespeare and it spelled out: 'Never, never, never, never, never.' He blamed several catastrophes in his life on things he had been writing at the time, including the malevolent *Crow*, the last poem of which he wrote days before the death of Assia Wevill. To Leonard Baskin in December 1969 — Assia had died in March — he wrote, 'I hope you haven't had a year of such poor luck as I've had. I'm half-inclined to suspect CROW.' According to a letter written in 1984:

> I stopped writing stories and radio plays etc in the 60s because I began to realise that each one foretold an episode in my life — sometimes in quite unbelievable physical detail. I did wonder if my writing such pieces actually brought them into existence.

He blamed the cancer that killed him on damage to his immune system incurred through writing his treatise *Shakespeare and the Goddess of Complete Being*. Most famously, though, he dreamed of a fox:

> ...in 1953, my second year at University, I was going through some kind of a crise... It became impossible to write a sentence, except in lucky moments. (It varied according to the author in question — I remember writing fluently about Blake.)... One night I sat up late writing & rewriting 3 or 4 lines I had managed to compose — the opening of an essay about Samuel Johnson (a personality I greatly liked). I left the page on my table and went to bed. Then I dreamed I was still sitting at my essay, in my usual agonising frame of mind, trying to get one word to follow another. The door opened, & a creature came in, with a fox's head, & a long skinny fox's body — but erect, & with human hands. He had escaped from a fire — the smell of burning hair was strong, & his skin was charred & in places cracking, bleeding freshly through the splits. He came across, & set his hand on the page & said: "Stop this. You are destroying us. He lifted his hand away, & the blood-print stayed on the page.

On the basis of this dream he changed his degree course to avoid writing critical prose. The impression is of a vision so entire, so complete in itself, that although it may seem incomprehensible to your average post-millennial atheist cosmopolitan, we must be forced to remember William Blake, or Milton. Hughes was, first and foremost, all about respecting the power of things that we humans can't understand. Poetry for him was intimately bound up with the body, which was bound up with the spirit. He was not shy of the word 'mystical'

This mysticism carried over into, or was deeply bound up with, his intimate relationship with wild animals. He always loved fishing, and the letters are full of long, intricate descriptions of fishing trips, fishing tackle, and fish caught — but he also rescued animals in trouble. This 1950 episode could have been written at any time (and indeed there is a letter to Frieda which tells her about his companionship with a hedgehog, albeit a happier one):

> ...out trundled a hedgehog, merry as you like, and obviously out for a good time. I thought he might make a jolly companion for an evening so I brought him in. After a while I noticed he had disappeared and later heard a noise just like the sobbing of a little child... I traced it to a pile of boxes and there was my comrade, with his nose pressed in a corner in a pool of tears, and his face all wet, and snivelling, and snuffling his heart out. I could have kissed him for compassion.

He ends, 'I carried sad Harry outside and let him go — he wouldn't even roll up he was so sad.' But characteristically, and with what looks like prescience, he also writes: 'It must be that they're something my affection can't touch, as though all my life the things I've loved best have been prickles towards that love, hedgehogs have become a symbol of such unrequitable desire...'

He also collected skulls, skins, teeth of dead badgers or foxes he found, not wanting 'God's artefacts' to be ground into the dust and forgotten — as he predicted they would be, with modern life all but forgetting them. He would write of sending someone an animal skull, as other people send a book or a bottle of wine. He writes:

My early life — first consciousness to age nine — revolved around my brother's world and the animals we searched for in it. I had a peculiar, obsessive relationship to wild creatures — simply their near presence… It's a physical reaction: like a kind of ecstasy….

The real jolt was my discovery of folklore… I became totally preoccupied — a mania — in collecting [folktales]… To me, it was the imaginative world that fitted into the natural world.

How our culture has changed, even in this short time, is summed up in his view — expressed in 1992 — that, 'Nowadays it's unthinkable that any child with an attentive mother who told… incessant stories… should remain unaware of folklore until thirteen years old.' I can hardly think of a child of my current acquaintance who is even aware of the *existence* of folklore, even recent European folklore. Having been that story-telling mother, I remember the books my own children were given by well-meaning friends: rewritten fairy tales where there is no magic and everyone has a happy ending. And the children these days are certainly not running around outside learning to skin a fox.

Hughes remained unusually sensitive to this creative, receptive state of childhood. His letters to his own children are alone worth the price of the book and should be given to teachers up and down the land. A letter he wrote in 1973 to Frieda, who had a school assignment to write a play about Cleopatra, would do for a creative writing text in any adult workshop even now, I should think. He simply demystifies the process of writing something, starting with the idea of researching it first: 'The best place to find out about Cleopatra is in a book, which every library possesses, called PLUTARCH'S LIVES… The one you must read is the *last half* of the life of *Antony*.' He continues, telling Frieda all about the sources, and what to find out, and advising her to get a map of Rome — he wouldn't be very impressed by a child who wasn't prepared to put some work into it — and then talks about writing notes:

> Before you write your play, write out — in notes — everything you can find, relating to Julius Caesar or Cleopatra or ancient Egypt, which you *think* you might somehow be able to drag into your play. Or film. Just jot a note. Even a couple of words, such as "Cleopatra's long nose". (She did have a long nose.)

> ...Then break the story up into *scenes*. As many as you like. (In Shakespeare's "Antony and Cleopatra" there must be 50 scenes. All he ever read was Plutarch's Lives.)

> ...Anyway, just you plough into it and mainly try to *make it interesting to yourself* — then it will be good.

His letters of the sixties are full of the need to provide a safe environment for his children so they could grow up untraumatised by, first, their mother's death and, second, the gaze of the prurient world. Many of the letters, to people who wanted to write about Sylvia Plath, are fiercely protective of the children. There is one even to Sylvia's mother when she proposed visiting soon after her death, where he warns her that her need to mourn Sylvia, applied to the children via doting (as 'your feelings for Sylvia, like mine, no longer have any worldly object'), would only harm them, would 'cripple their sense of reality and falsify their nature.'

The hugeness of this issue — the bigness of the Plath myth — is such that it is impossible to think of Ted Hughes without at some level accessing some feeling about Sylvia. The story of Assia Wevill compounds this to a point of, in my case, mystification. In the letter to Leonard Baskin quoted above he mentions 'back luck' but it seems that it must be more than that — one is bad luck, as Lady Bracknell might say, but two looks like carelessness — or, given the emphasis on deeper forces (combined, I suppose, with modern relationship theories), it looks like something not being how it should be within Hughes himself.

But in the early days the letters he wrote to Plath are marked by tenderness, care and passion: his 'Puss-Kish,' his 'Ponk,' writing of her 'ponky warmth,' signing 'love love love love love, Ted.' He wrote: 'Oh Sylvia. Where are you? I could crush you into my pores.'

The next seven years are full of letters either to her, or about her and their life together, to various family members — he wrote long, personal letters to her mother, Aurelia. It is clear how tightly joined the two were in their poetic purpose as well as their marriage. As to the state of the marriage — well, the old adage goes that no one can know about a marriage except for the two people in it, and these letters don't change that. They provide much that is suggestive, instructive, even inspirational; the level of passion may make you question the depth of your own, which would also be a mistake, such is the power of the myth — but after all, what happened happened, and it is not possible for us to know why.

To his sister Olwyn he wrote, days after Sylvia's death: 'Dear Olwyn, On Monday morning, at about 6 a.m., Sylvia gassed herself. … She asked me for help, as she so often has. I was the only person who could have helped her, and the only person so jaded by her states and demands that I could not recognise when she needed it. I'll write more later.'

To Aurelia Plath, a month later, he wrote:

I shall never get over the shock and I don't particularly want to. …I don't want ever to be forgiven. I don't mean that I shall become a public shrine of mourning and remorse, I would sooner become the opposite. But if there is an eternity, I am damned in it. Sylvia was one of the greatest truest spirits alive, and in her last months she became a great poet, and no other woman poet except Emily Dickinson can begin to compare with her, and certainly no living American.

So now I shall look after Frieda and Nick and you are not to worry about them.

Once the Plath legend became entrenched in syllabuses and books began being written, Hughes wrote letter after letter to their authors — including, in a really remarkable long letter, his and Sylvia's friend Al Alvarez — chiding them in no uncertain terms for their (admittedly unavoidable) skewing of events and begging them to desist. The letter to Alvarez is shocking in its visceral desperation.

The relationship that seems most disastrous as a relationship is the one with Assia Wevill, with whom Hughes argued and nearly broke up, got back together and argued again for six years — writing her letters that seem almost abject in their insistence that this relationship was important, real, fundamental, even while she dithered about her husband, David Wevill. The catastrophe of her suicide — and its attendant killing of their four-year-old daughter Shura — stunned Hughes into silence. Unlike in 1963, there are few letters in the book from the months after Assia's death, and certainly not many that discuss it. He did write, 'If I could have only given her hope in slightly more emphatic words in that last phone conversation.' And, in a characteristically frank letter to Sylvia's mother:

I'm sorry I haven't been communicative through this last ghastly year. It has been a struggle to do anything at all, I have lost every single battle. Fortunately Frieda and Nick are in good shape, doing well at school, healthy and all that I could wish...

I shall make another attempt now to get away from this house which has gradually become a hell for me — of paralysis and apathy as well as other things. Assia and I thought some atonement could be made for Sylvia, but this house saw that we were dragged into the utmost nightmare.

This last horror has taught me one thing. Sylvia's death threw my whole nature negative.

To Leonard Baskin he wrote: 'I have two nice children who make life a great pleasure. They come to the States every summer. I had a third, a little marvel, but she died with her mother.'

Fifteen years later in 1984 he wrote to Lucas Myers: 'I keep writing this and that, but it seems painfully little for the time I spend pursuing it. I wonder sometimes if things might have gone differently without the events of 63 & 69. I have an idea of those two episodes as steel doors shutting down over great parts of myself, leaving me that much less, just what was left, to live on. No doubt a more resolute artist would have penetrated the steel doors — but I believe big physical changes happen at these times, big self-anaesthesias.'

Regardless of his idea of himself as a less than 'resolute artist,' Hughes wrote and wrote, and wrote about his writing, to an astonishing degree over the coming years, as well as spending a large amount of time and energy looking after Plath's literary estate, even though he was moving 'through the stomach of the crocodile'. The seventies through to the nineties are the years when his letters go back to what they had been before: he was happily married to his second wife, Carol Orchard, was happily settled, writing and farming in Devon, became Poet Laureate. There are wonderful letters about his decision to publish *Birthday Letters*, about his early experiences of writing, about his theories about literature, his ideas about the spirit. There is all the gossipy stuff you want, where he slates someone in a letter to one person and then writes a friendly, open letter to that person. Hs remarks and summings-up of people are acid, often very funny, and true. He makes his plans and initiates projects and watches like a Rottweiler over his children, clearly enjoying their company as adults. He has his ideas, and brings them forward towards the 21st century. He is a bit of a crank: an authentic, original, genius crank.

There is a whole letter nearly two pages long (but possibly never sent), about how everybody writes differently on 'wordprocessors': 'Because handwriting is basically drawing of images (that's how graphologists read it — they decode the images in the various letters…) it engages not only the whole record of your psychological history (as your unique handwriting does) but it engages from word to word all the preverbal activities of your brain (as drawing images does), which then bring the (non-verbal) associative contribution to bear on what is being written about, and therefore help to determine the sequence of ideas and expressions, tones and rhythms etc… So beware. I'm going to get all that proved if I can get some brain-scanning specialist to do the experiments.'

There are letters here to other poets, to partners in projects, a 12-page (in this large-paged volume) letter to a French PhD student; letters to reviewers, to people interested in Plath, to unpublished poets, to family and old friends. In 1976, talking about the title of his collection *Gaudete*, he wrote a postscript panegyric to the folk-rock band Steeleye Span. The final letter in the book is to his aunt, Hilda Farrar, describing being awarded an Order of Merit by the Queen. The letter, which neglects to mention how ill he in fact is, includes a detailed drawing of the medal itself. He died nine days later.

This book is the first step in what will undoubtedly be a long process of bringing Ted Hughes' correspondence to light. Less than ten years after the man's death is soon enough to make reading the letters feel a bit intrusive, even while people have been generous in sharing them. Christopher Reid talks in his introduction of the many painful, often arbitrary, choices he had to make as to what to include: what he has achieved here is to bring the man vibrantly, poignantly, invigoratingly to life. Eventually there will be a need for the *Collected Letters*. In the meantime this is a book that everybody who's interested in interesting things should read.

THE DYLAN THOMAS QUESTION

This afternoon I'm part of a panel discussion at the London Welsh Centre in Gray's Inn Road, talking about Dylan Thomas to mark the beginning of his centenary year. The talk is being run by Rack Press (which has feet in both Wales and Bloomsbury) as part of the Bloomsbury Festival.

I was surprised to be asked to speak about Dylan Thomas, but I said yes because it seemed like a good chance to confront the problem. It felt like a problem, and I think there is a sort of Dylan Thomas Question, a knotty thing to be disentangled... I felt a bit bad about feeling this way until I read Seamus Heaney's essay in *The Redress of Poetry*, where he approaches Thomas from exactly the same position. He begins, 'Dylan Thomas is by now as much a case history as a chapter in the history of poetry', and lists a 'multi-channel set of associations': 'Thomas the Voice, Thomas the Booze, Thomas the Debts, Thomas the Jokes, Thomas the Wales, Thomas the Sex, Thomas the Lies...'

Like most of us — I suspect — I read Dylan Thomas voraciously as a teenager, drunk on the sounds and not really getting a word of it. No, okay, that's an exaggeration. I can remember the mad exhilaration of 'The force that through the green fuse drives the flower/drives my green age': the sounds, the inverted syntax, the working out of the metaphor which is half abstraction and half conceit... The rhyme schemes — the in-&-back-out rhyme of 'Prologue' — the diamonds on the page, the records my mother used to play us, with that voice... I'm a bit unfashionable. I love his voice and even his reading style. It's good old-fashioned declamation, it's poetry with no apologies for itself, and it comes from a much deeper place than that contemporary scourge, the 'poetry voice'. Even now if I read certain of his poems, they enter my brain — or rather, are activated — in the ringing tones of a natural poet and a natural orator.

I read him over and over, I read biographies of him, I read that book, *Dylan Thomas in America*. I knew there was also a John Malcolm Brinnin Question. When I arrived in London at 19 — the age he was when 'And Death shall Have No Dominion' was published — one of the first books I bought was Caitlin Thomas' angry memoir, *Leftover Life to Kill*. Needless to say, I was a bit in love with Dylan, but I was firmly on Caitlin's side. There was real pain in the fact that my birthplace, New York, was the bad guy in this story. My Uncle Pete told me during this teenage phase that he had been drinking with Dylan Thomas in the White Horse — along with half the city, apparently, and if they weren't there, they said they were — and since Uncle Pete knew absolutely everybody, I believed it.

And then eventually it just got too much about the story, and the declamation started to feel like a shtick, and the poems stopped working. I just gradually stopped reading Dylan Thomas. So this panel discussion has been a good chance to re-engage with a ghost. I've spent my week with the ghost, reading his poems, and Heaney's essay, and a vivid, passionate book review by John Berryman, and smaller things by Randall Jarrell — 'Dylan Thomas is very Welsh (he reminds me a little of Owen Glendower)' — and the ever-unforgiving Ian Hamilton.

In fact, everyone is agreed what the crux of the Dylan Thomas Problem is. Here's Randall Jarrell:

> If poetry were nothing but texture, Thomas would be as good as any poet alive. The what of his poems is hardly essential to their success, and the best and most brilliantly written pieces usually say less than the worst.

But at least this time the problem is about the poems, not the myth of the man (who sounds by all accounts an utter nightmare — I had his *Letters* but finally sold them last year, just too depressing). Dylan wrote in a letter (sold by me, quoted by Heaney): 'I think poetry should work from words, from the substance of words and the rhythm of substantial words set together, not towards words.' This can be read almost as his artistic manifesto; it encapsulates both his strength and his weakness. Heaney speaks of an 'almost autistic enclosure within the phonetic element', and cites Eliot's remark describing someone-or-other as 'a case of technical development proceeding ahead of spiritual development'. Certainly, I knew even at 14 that to Dylan Thomas the sounds were paramount. They were thrilling, and reading them again this week they've thrilled afresh. I only wish I'd been as diligent with metrics as he was at that age. Don Paterson has written in several essays that 'sound is sense'. He means it literally: that the sound of the poem and the meaning of the poem are one and the same. It's impossible not to think of that dictum when reading this:

And death shall have no dominion.
Dead men naked they shall be one
With the man in the wind and the west moon;
When their bones are picked clean and the clean bones gone,
They shall have stars at elbow and foot;
Though they go mad they shall be sane,
Though they sink through the sea they shall rise again;
Though lovers be lost love shall not;
And death shall have no dominion.
And death shall have no dominion.
Under the windings of the sea... [&c.]

This poem, published in the poet's teens, is a point where the Dylan

Thomas Question looms large, in all its paradox. Because this poem has everything. It has absolutely everything. Just speak those words. Go on. And Death shall have No Dominion...

It can't be read in any tones other than ringing ones. His language actually functions as musical notation. Look at lines three and four:

> With the MAN in the WIND and the WEST MOON;
> When their BONES are PICKED CLEAN and the CLEAN BONES GONE...

These are very unusual, written in anapaests and spondees, and they tell you how to read them, where the emphasis goes. The phonetic structure — which controls the passage of air through the throat and mouth, and the speed with which that happens, and the register in which it happens — functions almost like singing instructions. His technical aspects are flawless; his imagery is both startling and reminiscent of Shakespeare or the Metaphysicals; the repetition of that main line is just staggeringly effective. As Jarrell says, 'anyone interested in poetry will read [him]'.

But the poem goes on, and even while it grows in its rhetorical stature and imagery — 'Though they be mad and dead as nails,/ Heads of the characters hammer through daisies' — it becomes more and more abstract, and there is a dawning realisation: this is a poem is that is — despite what it says — also trying to imagine what death might be. 'Death' is a big word; but, like 'love', it means different things to different people and in different circumstances. This is heroic teenage boy poetry. He might as well be writing it about Alexander the Great. It's beautiful, and — as Jarrell says — successful. But it isn't having to struggle very hard against the dead weight of the dead hand of death-in-life and life-in-death. His most beloved people are not on the other side of the wall. if anything, this poem conveniently pretends that its ignorance is a kind of knowledge. Which maybe it is, thinking about it; it is a kind of innocence, a wishful thinking that nevertheless leads to a psychic truth, anyway.

Elsewhere in his lecture Heaney talks about phrase from Eavan Boland (in an essay in *PN Review* about Elizabeth Bishop): 'the suffered world'. Boland wrote: 'Poetic tone... is not a matter of the aesthetic of any one poem. It grows more surely, more painfully, from the ethics of the art. Its origins must always be in a suffered world rather than a conscious craft'. It is this suffered world that Heaney feels is the lacking element in Thomas' work — up to a point. If the dead do not die windily, one might be tempted to say there's certainly a lot of wind around them here. And the abstractions — as Berryman points out in his review, 'the key words: blood, sea, dry, ghost, grave, straw, worm, double, crooked, salt, cancer, tower, shape, fork, marrow, ... death, light, time, sun, night, wind, love, grief' — each of which appears 'many times and has regularly one or several symbolic values' — do stand in a universal, rather than a personal, position. His premises are more rhetorically established than hard-won spiritual triumphs.

But this is the starting point, not the solution. It's only the question, not the answer. And the symbolism is no accident; it was Thomas himself who first coined the idea of 'the Rimbaud of Cwmdonkin Drive'. Heaney comes down on the side of Thomas, in the end, partly on account of 'Do Not Go Gentle', which does resist a real suffered world; but Ian Hamilton takes the opposite view, agreeing strongly with The Problem and then predicting sourly that had he lived he'd have been all over the telly. (I know: eh?)

John Berryman, in his posthumous collection of essays *The Freedom of the Poet* (1976), reviews Thomas' 1940 collection, *The World I*

Breathe. This is what Jarrell was also reiewing; where Jarrell gave it one paragraph in a group review, Berryman gave it a considered few pages. The review is called 'Dylan Thomas: the Loud Hill of Wales'. But he pays forensically close attention to the poems, and defends them mightily. It's a fascinating fly-on-the-wall moment, a thorough, inquiring look at Dylan Thomas before his reputation was assured. He writes at length about Thomas' 'wealth of diction' — his 'unmistakable signature' — examining the words themselves in a great long list that takes up almost a page: 'blood, sea, dry, ghost, grave, straw, worm, double, crooked, salt, cancer, tower, shape, fork, marrow...' He cites 'one or several symbolic values', 'unusual epithets', compound words, colours (especially green), and words 'old, new, obsolete, coined, and colloquial'. He writes, 'Some of the language is Biblical. But the principle sources of imagery are the sea and sex'.

One Julian Symonds had written disparagingly in *The Kenyon Review* of Thomas' poems, 'that the seasons change; that we decrease in vigour as we grow older; that life has no meaning; that love dies. His poems mean no more than that. They mean too little.' Berryman robustly routs him, writing, 'I have not time to notice any considerable part of Symons' nonsense; one quotation must serve':

> Evidently it is necessary to point out to Symonds what is elementary, that a poem means more than the abstract, banal statement of its theme: it means its imagery, the disparate parts and relations of it, its ambiguities, by extension the techniques which produced it and the emotions it legitimately produces... there is a value and a meaning which cannot appear in Symons' catalogue. Even the single lines mean more than their prose doubles:

> *The fruit of man unwrinkles in the stars.*
> *Glory cracked like a flea.*

Sigh long, clay cold, lie shorn.
The terrible world my brother bares his skin.

I'd like simply to type out Berryman's essay and give it to you. He says: One has the sense of words set at an angle... a new language'. He cites 'certain technical derivations' (I might keep that phrase and use it), 'despite one's impressions of originalty'. These come, among others, from Blake, Yeats, Hopkins — obviously — and even early Auden. He wonders about possible roots in Welsh folk poetry.

Dylan Thomas didn't speak Welsh, but this last idea carries the weight of a truth. You don't need to speak a language to be influenced by it, if you are part of a culture that was formed out of that language and hear it all around you. Both the Welsh language and Dylan Thomas are full of rich consonantal sound and very expressive vowels. In his 2003 *Arena* programme about Dylan Thomas, Nigel Williams talked about this rhetorical style, too, saying Thomas clearly picked it up from everywhere: from the preachers in Swansea, from the air. Though this style of preaching has almost died out, he described Thomas as having the very Welsh (i.e., untranslatable) quality of *hwyl*.

So here we are. It's the beginning of the centenary year. The questions are hovering, the position is stated, and it's a starting point. I was very struck this week, looking for things to read, that in my half a wall of poetry criticism there were only these four things to read. Maybe everyone got sick of all the histrionics, but no one's writing about him. There's space for a feminist essay on Thomas the Patriarchy, certainly — and also one on Thomas the Earth Goddess. Thomas the Body. He wrote in a letter, quoted again by Heaney:

All thoughts and actions emanate from the body. Therefore the description — however abstruse it may be — can be beaten home by bringing it on to a physical level. Every idea, intuitive or intellectual, can be imaged and translated in terms of the body, its flesh, blood, sinews, veins, glands, organs, cells and senses. Through my small bone island I have learnt all I know, experienced all, and sensed all.

There's also Thomas the Radio, Thomas the Childhood, Thomas the Kitsch. I'd love to read about Thomas the Technique, something like Berryman's approach applied to the whole work. You could almost take these headings and commission a critical anthology...

MAN OF JAZZ AND CONSCIENCE
MACNEICE'S *AUTUMN JOURNAL*

In 1963, after Louis MacNeice's premature death from pneumonia, Philip Larkin wrote that 'his poetry was the poetry of our everyday life, of shop-windows, traffic policemen, ice-cream soda, lawn-mowers, and an uneasy awareness of what the news-boys were shouting . . . he displayed a sophisticated sentimentality about falling leaves and lipsticked cigarette stubs: he could have written the words of 'These Foolish Things'.' Larkin was a famous jazz buff, so this is not the pejorative it might have been in the hands of a critic like — for example — Ian Hamilton, who wrote of MacNeice's 'love of bright particulars', saying he 'loved the surface but lacked the core'.

Louis MacNeice is utterly a poet we imagine lighting a cigarette, catching a movie, arriving at a party. This is not the same thing as not having a core. People who knew him reported that although he was always *in* the pub, he was not *of* the pub; that he was highly social but kept himself aloof; but this is the condition of the observer/reporter.

MacNeice's long poem *Autumn Journal*, which describes the daily personal, social, and political life he lived in London during the decent into the Second World War, was written as reportage, in real time. It stands now as possibly his major achievement. His introspective bent gave him a capacity almost unique among his contemporaries for realising how intertwined the political, cultural, and personal lives are — the most important events still being made up of silly little ('foolish') things.

One autumn, with dangerously high pressure in my glaucoma-ridden left eye, I reread *Autumn Journal* at the rate of about one section every two days. I had been told by a consultant at Moorfields Eye Hospital that if the pioneering laser surgery they were going to use on it didn't work, I would need surgery — which, due to specific conditions in my eye, "would carry a significant risk of complications". The doctor said: "You know what that means?" It was a euphemism, of course. I went through my bad autumn alongside MacNeice in his autumn of 1938, reading within a stone's throw of (and sometimes actually in) the places he describes. There was a lot at stake for both of us, in our parallel autumns.

While I looked forward to pain, uncertainty and the possible loss of sight, the poet said goodbye to a love, and prepared himself psychologically for war. His affair with Nancy Coldstream (née Sharp, later Spender) ended that autumn, and in 1939 his divorce would also be final.

Autumn Journal stands as a time capsule, a 56-page moment in which the reader just knows what it was like to be alive, in London, in those few months. MacNeice is worldly and, though jaded, full of appetite for the moment. The poem is as subjective as this reading of it. (He writes in his prefatory note, '... poetry in my opinion must be honest before anything else and I refuse to be 'objective' or clear-cut at the cost of honesty.') *Autumn Journal* is consummately honest. It was written practically in the moment: there was no time to reflect and repackage things into something more palatable; even when Barcelona fell, after the poem was completed but before it was published, MacNeice left the manuscript as it was, a moment in time.

In his prefatory note he writes: 'I am aware that there are overstatements in this poem — e.g. in the passages dealing with Ireland, the Oxford by-election or my own more private existence ...

if I had been writing a didactic poem proper, it would have been my job to qualify or eliminate these overstatements and inconsistencies. But I was writing what I have called a Journal ... It is the nature of this poem to be neither final nor balanced. I have certain beliefs which, I hope, emerge in the course of it but which I have refused to abstract from the context. For this reason I shall probably be called a trimmer by some and a sentimentalist by others'.

However reserved he was in company, MacNeice's life and his feelings are in the foreground of his verse. In those months he felt the international crisis in light of his personal crisis, and vice versa.

In 1937, in *Modern Poetry: a Personal Essay*, MacNeice had written: 'I would have a poet able bodied, fond of talking, a reader of the newspapers, capable of pity and laughter, informed in economics, appreciative of women, involved in personal relationships, actively interested in politics, susceptible to physical impressions'. This description fits the poet of *Autumn Journal* to a T. In fact, on 7 February, 1939, Eliot wrote to MacNeice that this was the strength of the poem: 'I have read through *Autumn Journal*, and I think it is very good indeed. At times I was much moved, and what is still more unusual in the case of a single long poem, I found that I read it through without my interest flagging at any point. That is due partly to the dexterity with which you vary the versification, and, I think, to the fact that the imagery is all imagery of things lived through...'

Around November, Eliot wrote to MacNeice asking for a statement about the poem to use in the catalogue, as *Autumn Journal* was slated for spring publication. The resulting statement is a perfect description of the poem, and very interesting; it shows both the extent to which the poem was conceived in toto and then written, and the extent of MacNeice's self-awareness: it's impressive for a poet to give so accurate an external description of his own work — a work not yet even written.

Autumn Journal:

A long poem from 2,000 to 3,000 lines written from August to December 1938. Not strictly a journal but giving the tenor of my emotional experiences during that period.
It is about everything which from first-hand experience I consider important.
It is written in sections averaging about 80 lines in length. This division gives it a dramatic quality, as different parts of myself (e.g. the anarchist, the defeatist, the sensual man, the philosopher, the would-be good citizen) can be given their say in turn.
It contains rapportage [sic], metaphysics, ethics, lyrical emotion, autobiography, nightmare.
balanced by pictures.
Places presented include Hampshire, Spain, Birmingham, Ireland, & — especially — London.
It is written throughout in an elastic kind of quatrain. This form (a) gives the whole poem a formal unity but (b) saves it from monotony by allowing it a great range of appropriate variations.
The writing is direct; anyone could understand it.
I think this is my best work to date; it is both a panorama and a confession of faith."

The poem opens with a powerful vision of normality in the shires — tinged with warning. It's August, and MacNeice sits on a train whose movement toward the city and the future is inexorable, although it is also for the moment an interlude. This section sets up the First War as backdrop to the peaceful — and hard-won — gentility that is about to be blown apart again by the next one:

Close and slow, the summer is ending in Hampshire,
  Ebbing away down ramps of shaven lawn where close-clipped yew
Insulates the lives of retired generals and admirals
  And the spyglasses hung in the hall and the prayer-books ready in the
                              pew
  And the sunflowers' Salvation Army blare of brass
And the spinster sitting in a deck-chair picking up stitches
  Not raising her eyes to the noise of the 'planes as they pass...

And, after talking of '... all the inherited assets of bodily ease / and all the inherited worries, rheumatism and taxes, / and whether Stella will marry and what to do with Dick', all the reassuring convention that we now know only from novels, he goes straight into a present that presages the future:

And I am in the train now too and summer is going
  South as I go north
Bound for the dead leaves falling, the burning bonfire,
  The dying that brings forth
The harder life, revealing the trees' girders,
  The frost that kills the germs of *laissez-faire*;
West Meon, Tisted, Farnham, Woking, Weybridge,
  Then London's stale and packed and pregnant air.

This litany invokes all the people who must also face the threat — 'the harder life' — together. The key phrase may be 'the germs of *laissez-faire*': Edna Longley, in her book *Louis MacNeice: A Study*, expands on this: 'The term *laissez-faire* recurs throughout *Autumn Journal*, and it covers economic, political, and moral sins of omission. Outworn modes of thought as well as of behaviour contribute to laissez-faire'. This includes, as we shall see, the outworn modes of thought and behaviour of the people in the houses.

London is indeed pregnant with something throughout the poem. Its physical presence is strong, and the depredations on it cause MacNeice an almost physical pain.

> ... Hitler yells on the wireless,
>> The night is damp and still
> And I hear dull blows on wood outside my window;
>> They are cutting down the trees on Primrose Hill.
> The wood is white like the roast flesh of chicken,
>> Each tree falling like a closing fan;
> No more looking at the view from seats beneath the branches,
>> Everything is going to plan.
>> (from Section VII)

MacNeice was so depressed by this tree-chopping that the next day he went to stay with a friend. Even now there are no trees on the top of Primrose Hill.

This section ends by sweeping us down the escalator into the troubled final months of 1938 – and beyond. The tonal shifts in this section – weary detachment giving onto felt love and grief, giving onto anger and dread and other feelings almost too fleeting to notice – encapsulate the tones of the several themes of this poem.

> And the train's rhythm becomes the ad nauseam repetition
>> Of every tired aubade and maudlin madrigal,
> The faded airs of sexual attraction
>> Wandering like dead leaves along a warehouse wall:
> 'I loved my love with a platform ticket,
>> A jazz song,
> A handbag, a pair of stockings of Paris Sand;
>> I loved her long . . .
> With my office hours, with flowers and sirens,
>> With my budget, my latchkey and my daily bread'.

This description of the manner of love, and its jazz, are both evocative of the whole texture of the poem, and its debt to the atmosphere and rhythms of jazz. The London MacNeice lived in that autumn was full of sex, cigarette smoke, drink, and music for dancing:

> In Tottenham Court Road the tarts and negroes
> > Loiter beneath the lights
> And the breeze gets colder as on so many other
> > September nights.

Jazz's improvisation, looseness of syntax and beat, are everywhere in this poem. Written at speed as events unfolded, in run-on sentences, lists, changes of register and piled-up subject matter, *Autumn Journal* is, in large part, a riff. Parts of it make almost no sense if you try, like a Victorian schoolmistress, to parse them out. The poem works against that aesthetic as it flows and swirls.

The closer the poet gets to his destination, the more the personal and general are mixed together. It's still technically summertime, but events and hard reality are upon us. It's time to let go of a lover and hang on to a society: 'That we cannot make any corner in life or in life's beauty, / That no river is a river which does not flow.' This idea of a river — a river in spate — is central to the poem. It recurs in several contexts, including metaphorical:

> And so to London and down the ever-moving Stairs
> > Where a warm wind blows the bodies of men together
> And blows apart their complexes and cares.

MacNeice suffered all his life with nightmares, from the time when he was five and his mother was taken away to the asylum, never to return. 'Spider, spider, twisting tight—' he writes, in Section II; 'but the watch is wary beneath the pillow— / I am afraid in the web of the night . . . *Noli me tangere*, my soul is forfeit.'

As he wrote to Eliot, the structure of the poem allows his different personae each to get a say, and the nightmare monologue of Section II also contains, like the overture of an opera, many of the motifs that follow. The poem's continuous counterpoint of day and night, light and dark, echoes the poem's seesawing between the poet's temperamental optimism and a pessimism which may also be temperamental but is also based on external circumstances. Throughout the poem night is falling, or day is dawning, neither trustworthy — each always presages the other. The coming day prevail, but night gets the last scene.

The nighttime fear at the beginning enacts the 'worries and cares' that the War, of course, cannot really blow apart — except to blow open. It places the entire narrative within the context of MacNeice's hidden terrors. The poem's almost stream-of-consciousness monologue gives us the parts of MacNeice — 'the anarchist, the defeatist, the sensual man, the philosopher, the would-be good citizen' — one after another, as in this passage.

> I wonder now whether anything is worth
> > The eyelid opening and the mind recalling.
> And I think of Persephone gone down to dark,
> > No more a virgin, gone the garish meadow,
> But why must she come back, why must the snowdrop mark
> > That life goes on forever?

The semi-didacticism of *Autumn Journal* is personal, in keeping with the feeling that 'it is difficult to speak for oneself without speaking for others or to speak for others without speaking for oneself'. Over and again MacNeice describes the terrible cost the 'status quo' (a condition caused by the culpable laziness of laissez-faire) exacts of ordinary people. The rich, seething life of the city is lived by people ('the slaves') who are not reaping the rewards of the system. Of course, these very people need to be spurred on to action to prevent the final disaster, the loss of even the freedom to live their tedious lives. It is ordinary people who will be killed in the ensuing war; it is ordinary people who voted for Chamberlain and enabled the disaster of the Munich agreement.

So people come back from holiday and resume their precious, but mundane – precious *because* mundane – lives:

> Now the till and the typewriter call the fingers,
>> The workman gathers his tools
> For the eight-hour day but after that the solace
>> Of films or football pools...

This life is everywhere questioned. MacNeice duly goes back to work, teaching classics – 'term is again beginning' – and explores the big questions of thirties politics: the system of privilege, and his place in it, the extent to which the 'system' can give everybody 'a place in the sun'. While he is absolutely an ordinary, not special, person in this churning London, MacNeice is aware that, as an educated, middle-class person with reputation and contacts, he also enjoys a privileged status, and is unflinchingly critical of his own hypocrisies:

> ... an utterly lost and daft
> System that gives a few at fancy prices
>> Their fancy lives
> While ninety-nine in the hundred who never attend the banquet
>> Must wash the grease of ages off the knives.

The classical education, first received and now imparted by MacNeice, and which is so integral to how he perceives and navigates the world, is a large part of this uneasy self-image. It both signifies and embodies the hypocrisy of society, and is the means by which he is able to see, and say it. This paradox enables some of the best irony in the poem.

> But certainly it was fun while it lasted
>> And I got my honours degree
> And was stamped forever as a person of intelligence and culture
>> For ever wherever two or three
> Persons of intelligence and culture
>> Are gathered together in talk
> Writing definitions on invisible blackboards
>> In non-existent chalk.

MacNeice questions his own motives and appearances as much as, if not more than, the next person's. Unlike his more comfortably didactic friend W.H. Auden, he can't articulate any simple formulation of 'the truth':

> And the individual, powerless, has to exert the
>> Powers of will and choice
> And choose between enormous evils, either
>> Of which depends on somebody else's voice.

After the blind faith of the slaughtered generation of 1914-18, this is the modern conscience: the private man testing his position. Even Auden later came a cropper on that issue with his poem 'September 1, 1939', with its line, 'we must love one another or die.' After the war he changed it to 'we must love one another *and* die' (my italics); still later he excised it from his collected works, saying it was the most dishonest thing he had ever written. MacNeice's world is always, as in his famous poem 'Snow,' 'incorrigibly plural,' and this is very much the world of *Autumn Journal*.

So structurally embedded is this plurality that without it there could be no *Autumn Journal*. The sections, alternating between political, life, local colour, the past, the inner life, are an argument MacNeice conducts with himself. Section VIII opens with a graphic description of a quotidian complacency, himself in the starring role eight years previously. It was the depression years, and:

> The steaks were tender, the films were fun,
>> The walls were striped like a Russian ballet,
> There were lots of things undone,
>> But nobody cared, for the days were early.
> . . . We slept in linen, we cooked with wine,
>> We paid in cash and took no notice
> Of how the train ran down the line
>> Straight into the sun against the signal.

Here we have the warning of consequences. For one thing, the marriage broke down. In 1938 MaNeice is living in a rented flat with his small son and a disapproving nanny. Of his own circumstances he says, 'Sun shines easy but I no longer / Docket a place in the sun — / No wife, no ivory tower, no funk-hole'. And of the wider situation it all comes, in the end, to where 'the crisis is put off and things look better . . . / And stocks go up and wrecks / Are salved . . . only the Czechs / Go down and without fighting'.

Section IX goes further back than MacNeice's own past. Back at work ('Now we are back to normal') he is 'impresario of the Ancient Greeks'. The tone of his voice in this section is almost as hard to catch as dapples of sunlight on stone, moving between straight statement, irony, satire, self-accusation and a sort of incredible tiredness. 'Conscious — long before Engels — of necessity / And therein free / They plotted out their life with truism and humour / Between the jealous gods and the callous sea', he writes:

And for a thousand years they went on talking,
        Making such apt remarks,
A race no longer of heroes but of professors
        And crooked business men and secretaries and clerks
Who turned out dapper little elegiac verses
        On the ironies of fate, the transience of all
Affections, carefully shunning the overstatement
        But working the dying fall.

Of course he is talking, here, about the cognoscenti, the purveyors of the 'definitions on invisible blackboards in invisible chalk'. This irony, always present and sometimes in the ascendant, eventually crystallises into a sort of double bluff that seems to ironise itself:

And the trimmers at Delphi and the dummies at Sparta and lastly
        I think of the slaves.
And how one can imagine oneself among them
        I do not know.
It was all so unimaginably different
        And all so long ago.

But as *Autumn Journal* itself tells us over and over, *everything* is unimaginably different. You can't expect the past to solve anything — just as you can't expect the future to solve it.

The ever-present present has its moment in the Oxford by-election — critical to the outcome of the crisis — at which MacNeice volunteered to drive voters to the polls: a call for small, ordinary actions by small, ordinary people. 'What is the use / Of asking what is the use of one brick only?' 'That Rome was not built in a day is no excuse / For *laissez-faire*, for bowing to the odds against us...' It has been pointed out that this is the only place in the poem where MacNeice actually *does* anything (though this seems a little unfair).

Here he is, driving home dejectedly after the election of the pro-Munich Tory candidate, Lord Hailsham:

Dawn and London and daylight and last the sun:
    I stop the car and take the yellow placard
Off the bonnet; that little job is done
    Though without success or glory.
The plane-tree leaves come sidling down
    (Catch my guineas, catch my guineas)
And the sun caresses Camden Town,
    The barrels of oranges and apples.

This passage seems to hint at a London just as much apocryphal as it is really-here. The barrels of oranges and apples echo the 'oranges and lemons' of the Bells of St. Clements in the old rhyme about London's medieval churches. This nursery-rhyme element comes up in other places too — in MacNeice's device of repetition or refrain, in some of his phraseology — and underlines the absolutely basic everyday quality (the poet had a small child at the time) of the experienced action.

But the apple-cart is upset, and people are hanging on the words of the newsboys ('... posters flapping on the railings tell the fluttered / World that Hitler speaks, that Hitler speaks / and we cannot take it in and we go to our daily / Jobs to the dull refrain of the caption 'War'...'), though they don't want to ('And we think 'This must be wrong, it has happened before, / Just like this, we must be dreaming'...').

This suffocating air of panic, or paralysis, pervades the poem, underlined by the breathless use of 'and', 'and', 'and'. Although the situation was rapidly, at that stage, crystallising itself, things weren't so clear-cut then as they now appear; Hitler and Mussolini had their supporters. The Holocaust was undreamt-of. Edna Longley says: 'The poem dramatises our full human alarm when historical forces move fast'. Like jazz itself, and like the jazzy extemporaneous hurtling lines the poem is written in – the alternate feminine endings impelling us to the next line, but the rhyme words themselves pragmatically short and simple), life issomething you can only make it up as you go along. MacNeice, for all his self-questioning, is clearly impatient of those – like the voters of Oxford – who can't, or who choose not to, see this.

> And they said "The man in the street is so naïve, he never
>> Can see the wood for the trees;
> He thinks he knows he sees a thing but cannot
>> Tell you how he knows the thing he thinks he sees."
> And oh how much I liked the Concrete Universal,
>> I never thought that I should
> Be telling them vice-versa
>> That they can't see the trees for the wood.

Section XV gives a form to the public reaction to the crisis, as well as MacNeice's private reaction to the entire *mise en scène*, including the breakdown of his love life. 'Shelley and jazz and lieder and love and hymn-tunes', he begins, 'And day returns too soon; / We'll get drunk among the roses / In the valley of the moon'. Desperate, maybe beneath the sign of Johnny Walker, who 'moves his legs like a cretin over Trafalgar Square', MacNeice hymns:

> Give me an aphrodisiac, give me lotus,
>> Give me the same again;
> . . .
>> Let the old Muse loosen her stays
> Or give me a new Muse with stockings and suspenders
>> And a smile like a cat,

With false eyelashes and finger-nails of carmine
    And dressed by Schiaparelli, with a pill-box hat.
...
Give us sensations and then again sensations —
    Strip-tease, fireworks, all-in wrestling, gin...

But this bender can't last:

Oh look who comes here. I cannot see their faces
    Walking in file, slowly in file
...
        Following the track from the gallows back to the town;
Each has a rope at the end of his neck. I wonder
        Who let these men come back, who cut them down;
And now they reach the gate and line up opposite
        The neon lights on the medieval wall
...
But something in their faces is familiar;
    Where have we seen them before?

The panic continues: 'But take no notice of them, out with the ukulele, / The saxophone and the dice; / They are sure to go away if we take no notice ;/ Another round of drinks or make it twice.' Here the nightmare dialogue woven through the poem comes into its own, takes over the action. It is MacNeice's nightmare, or complex, and also everybody's. 'You can't step into the same river twice,' he tells himself, 'so there can't be / Ghosts; thank God that rivers always flow. / Sufficient to the moment is the moment.' With the arrival of the ghosts that only he can see, MacNeice sets himself apart from the other drinkers, despising them although he knows he is like them.

    Give us another drink;
This little lady has a fetish,

> She goes to bed in mink.
> This little pig went to market—
>   Now, I think you may look, I think the coast is clear.
> Well, why don't you answer?
>   I can't answer because they are still there.

The accounts must be paid, the debits must be cleared. Barcelona, the rallying point and ideological hub of the intelligentsia's concerns, occupies two important sections of *Autumn Journal*. One deals with — again — the spectre of the past, and the second with the present. The first, Section VI, recounts a visit made just before the Spanish Civil War, with suggestions of a parallel between Barcelona then and London during 1938 — and the nothing-to-do-with-me passivity at work in both, as those who are doing all right in the moment can see no further:

> And we thought the papers a lark
>   With their party politics and blank invective;
> And we thought the dark
>   Women who dyed their hair should have dyed it more often.

This section ends with a reminder of what is to come. The trippers return 'home, forgetting Spain, not realising / That Spain would soon denote / Our grief, our aspirations; / Not knowing that our blunt / Ideals would find their whetstone, that our spirit / Would find its frontier on the Spanish front, / Its body in a rag-tag army.'

The penultimate section reprises this and finishes off the action with stark auguries for the coming year. MacNeice lists the deprivations of the Spaniards, much as he did in Section VI, but this time with more feeling; by now he knows this scenario is his own future, and it's in sight:

We have come to a place in space where shortly
        All of us may be forced to camp in time . . .
But still they manage to laugh
        Though they have no eggs, no milk, no fish, no fruit, no
                tobacco, no butter,
Though they live upon lentils and sleep in the Metro . . .
And it appears that every man's desire
        Is life rather than victuals.

MacNeice is feeling the cost this time — or feeling for it: 'Here at last the soul has found its voice' — and he examines his own reluctance, which is born of his roots in Ireland (with the history and dread of bloodshed) and his childhood during the Great War, and sees that he is in no way — along with everybody else ('We who play for safety, / A safety only in name') — exempted from the disaster at Munich:

I admit that for myself I cannot straiten
        My broken rambling track
Which reaches so irregularly back
        To burning cities and rifled rose-bushes
And cairns and lonely farms
        Where no one lives, makes love or begets children,
All my heredity and my upbringing
        Having brought me only to the Present's arms —
The arms not of a mistress but of a wrestler . . .
. . . I have loved defeat and sloth,
        The tawdry halo of the idle martyr;
I have thrown away the roots of will and conscience,
        Now I must look for both,
Not any longer act among the cushions
        The dying Gaul...

This 'dying Gaul', rhyming with the 'dying fall' he mocked in the ancient Greek poetasters, puts MacNeice himself retroactively into the frame in that previous section. Critics of the poem have seized on this diffidence, this self-accusation, to call the poem 'The Bourgeois' Progress', or to describe it as 'never very deep or certain in thought, rather too conspicuously elaborating the picture of an easy-going but attractive personality'. Today they might ridicule MacNeice as a mere *Guardian*-reader. But it's easy to go with the herd, and MacNeice — true to the habits instilled in him, no doubt, by the education he describes so vividly in *Autumn Journal* — is more of a *mensch* than that, I think, for examining his own motives. In Section XVI he writes:

Nightmare leaves fatigue:
      We envy men of action
Who sleep and wake, murder and intrigue
      Without being doubtful, without being haunted.
And I envy the intransigence of my own
      Countrymen who shoot to kill and never
See the victim's face become their own
      Or find his motive sabotage their motives.

Looping back to his childhood in Ireland: 'So reading the memoirs of Maud Gonne, / Daughter of an English mother and a soldier father, / I note how a single purpose can be founded on / A jumble of opposites'. Like his nightmares, this question of his Irishness, or his relative Englishness, plagued MacNeice all his life — caught as a child between the affiliations of his parents and the servants ('And one read black where the other read white, his hope / The other man's damnation'), and later when he was sent to be educated in England, where he lived most of his adult life. He ruefully concludes the whole section by calling Ireland (this will be one of those overstatements, then) 'a bore and a bitch':

And she gives her children neither sense nor money
        Who slouch around the world with a gesture and a brogue
And a faggot of useless memories.

The purpose of looking back for MacNeice personally was to enable him to move forward with grace. Over and again the poem warns of trying to base the future on the past; the necessity of doing just that, while at the same time not doing it, is one of the poem's sternest 'old conundrums'. (George Orwell: 'Nothing was more desolating at the beginning of this war than the way in which the whole of the older generation conspired to pretend that it was the war of 1914-18 all over again. All the old duds were back on the job, twenty years older, with the skull plainer in their faces'.)

It is this inability to be either one thing or the other, but both — of seeing both 'the wood for the trees' and 'the trees for the wood' — that ultimately defines this poem. This seeing is the core of its moral element. MacNeice, uncomfortable in his conscious enjoyment of relative privilege, was unequivocal about his horror in the face of the Munich agreement and the weight of shared responsibility for the body civic and politic. (Critics of MacNeice also usually forget to mention the anger that still smoulders in Britain against Auden, who wrote out his diffidence from the safety of 52nd St.

The final section, XXIV, opens with the word 'sleep': but it is a false sleep. 'Sleep, my body, sleep, my ghost,' he writes, 'Sleep, my parents and grand-parents, / And all those I have loved most: / One man's coffin is another man's cradle'. This is both lullaby and prayer for the old year, and a prayer in the spirit of the classic, 'If I should die before I wake'. He writes: 'Tonight we sleep / On the banks of the Rubicon':

Sleep serene, avoid the backward
    Glance; go forward, dreams, and do not halt
(Behind you in the desert stands a token
    Of doubt—a pillar of salt).

The poem ends, after all these exhortations (like those quitting smoke tapes you're supposed to listen to in your sleep), with an invocation of the day to come, the first day (as everyone expected) of the year when the war will start.

The two Barcelona sections are, for me at least, where MacNeice's self-questioning tendency comes closest to the mortal weakness his detractors claim; but vulnerability can be strength. These sections are central to his examination of his own attitude to the impending war. He took his 1938 trip to Spain largely so he would have 'copy' for his poem; he travelled via Paris, Christmased in some degree of style, and stayed at the Ritz in Barcelona, amid the shortages. He carried food with him, including some cognac and a salami.

In his unfinished autobiography, *The Strings are False*, MacNeice — not unaware of this aspect — writes:

> In December 1938 I accepted a suggestion that I should visit Barcelona in company with some other English writers. The other writers falling out or ill, I decided to go by myself, got a visa for Spain from the Spanish Consulate in London. — — was very disapproving, said I only wanted to go to Spain to show off. I answered that it was rather late in the day to show off in this way, as nearly all literary London had long ago done the rounds of the trenches in Madrid and hobnobbed with the Republican celebrities. I admitted, however, that my motives were egotistical; I was sensation-hunting, testing myself, eager to add a notch to my own history.

On New Year's Eve a bomb fell not far from the Ritz ('There had been eight minutes between the siren and the bombs, unusually long, plenty of time to take shelter but people had remained in the street thinking it was a raid on the port; the number of dead was not certain'); the next morning MacNeice walked out 'and came upon a milling crowd, thought it was a food queue, a riot, a political meeting, but no it was only the stamp collectors doing their Sunday morning swapping'. He visited shelters, bomb sites, schools, colonies for refugees. People kept cockerels, hens, even rabbits on their window balconies and he was woken by cock-crow at all hours. He describes the girls and women with high heels and lipstick.

And he goes home and writes: 'Listen: a whirr, a challenge, an aubade— / It is the cock crowing in Barcelona'. After the lullaby ends at the end of the poem, and we are left in bed to fall asleep, it is this cock-crow at the end of the previous section—the previous day—that still rings in the ears.

The year after this, just before MacNeice's 100th birthday, my father was in a nursing him in Connecticut. I went to see him at the end of August—the time of year when this poem begins. I had been warned not to expect much, and indeed he was foggy and confused. I told him I had been writing about MacNeice, and quick as a flash his eyes brightened and he said: "He was no WH Auden!"

I assured him that there was now a school of thought... Really, one of the best things about Auden was the way he interrogated himself over that one line in 'September 1 1939', changing the line to its opposite, and then realising both were true.

In the end I didn't go half-blind. I had twenty lasers to each eye, an accommodation which in the end didn't prevent the need for more invasive action. The route home from my visits to the clinic at Moorfields Eye Hospital took me through Shoreditch, past St.

Leonard's Hospital, where MacNeice died.

Reading *Autumn Journal* in the post-9/11 world, it was tempting to wonder what MacNeice would have made of things. What he might have written about the cartoon crisis, for example. What would he have made of our current readiness to curtail our civic freedoms? Or the way in which rhetoric, language itself, is being used to turn the electorate against itself? Ultimately each of us has a conscience, and it is how we use it — precisely, our right and responsibility to be democratic citizens — which is under discussion. MacNeice was a citizen, and a man of conscience, *par excellence*.

Afterword

Ian Hamilton, writing in 1973, said that MacNeice was a perfect poet for rediscovery by 'a generation of post-war poets for whom such bafflement represents the proper limits of political involvement and whose intermittent nostalgia for more vigorous public contexts can be quenched by his sharply documented local colour.' This is not only a bit odd, considering how politically engaged 1960s poetry was; it seems to me a cop-out. By making a demand of the work to be a particular thing, only to turn around and gleefully say it wasn't that thing, Hamilton merely exposed his own prejudices.

John Wilkinson in 2007 launched at poor old MacNeice the accusation of being 'the most influential agent of a middlebrow humanism for which ease and stability of reception constitutes an ethical good' — referring to him dismissively in that context as 'the BBC radio producer Louis MacNeice' — and of 'maundering.' This may sound like no more than what Hamilton said, but Wilkinson seems to consider MacNeice a snob, stuffy, an example of 'the reduced horizons of British and Irish poetry in the second half of the twentieth century.'

In the same essay he compares MacNeice unfavourably to Frank O'Hara, the point of comparison being their respective poems about the deaths of two popular entertainers: music hall artiste Florrie Forde, in MacNeice's case, and Billie Holliday in O'Hara's. The issue seems to be MacNeice's 'dismissive patrician' attitude: the opposite of Hamilton's beef. 'The Day Lady Died' is one of O'Hara's great poems; 'The Death of an Actress' is not quite as bad as Wilkinson makes out but certainly wouldn't have put MacNeice on the map. This comparison illustrates the danger of reading only by our current cultural lights. O'Hara was 'genuinely democratic,' and so, on his terms, was MacNeice; had he not had to earn a living at the BBC, he wouldn't have died from collecting sound effects for a radio play. MacNeice was democratic in a society that was less democratic than pop-obsessed 1950s New York. *Autumn Journal* is in fact about the shocks that his society suffered. Like O'Hara, MacNeice wrote to the quotidian life he lived.

MacNeice has proved to be the wellspring of a renaissance of Irish poetry. Poets, both Irish and non-Irish, now claim him as an influence. His immaculately raffish prosody is infinitely easier to work with than Auden's classical austerity. It suits the surface of life — that thing we are currently deluged under — and how it plays (or plays havoc) beneath. MacNeice insists that, among our rightful doubts and fears, we must remain true to a moral core, but he doesn't pretend to tell us what it is. He's a whole person: he has heart; he has sex; he has no fear of being seen walking around the streets in the rain trying to hail a cab, nor does he fear a wide frame of reference; he has a jolly nice overcoat; he has rhythm; he has music. Who could ask for anything more?

BEAUTY AND MEANING: FREE THE WORD!

'I would like, if I could, to bring into this, somewhere the unfashionable notion of 'Beauty', which I find compelling anf immediate, however theoretically inadequate.'
Ian Hamilton Finlay, letter to Pierre Garnier, 1963

It is a truth universally acknowledged that words set free from the treadmill of traditional printing can play in different ways. The signature shape in the ICA's current exhibition, *Poor. Old. Tired. Horse*, which launches from the concrete poetry of the fifties and sixties, is round.

The first room of the exhibition is dominated by Ian Finley Hamilton's gigantic red *Sea Poppy*, a wall-sized painted mandala of letter-and-number combinations, which turn out to be the codes for ships. As evocative, in its way, as Carol Ann Duffy's famous poem 'Finesterre', and almost unrecognisable on a full wall after seeing it in photographic reproduction.

In the first room Liliane Lijn's spinning cones, with words and characters dotted around them, spin on turntables. One is waist-high. Past those, the punning concentrics of Ferdinand Kriwet, which are embossed and painted like road-signs: 'SODOMESTICK SADOMASORRY'. What we say and what we mean, explored in a visual context of utilitarianism, they are funny, troubling and very satisfying. Elsewhere, Kriwet fills entire walls with giant sheets of acrylic given the same treatment, with rings of words acquiring and losing syntax depending on which word you start with.

This breaking down of accepted (or, depending how you looked at it, tired) modes of meaning is the top note of the fifties and sixties in art, and — like the psychedelic experience — is a synaesthesiac's delight. Bing too linear, too one-sense in your perceptions was seen as hampering your ability to understand: 'square'. The period was fuelled by a huge interest in non-western modes of thinking and perception, mysticism, Buddhism, meditation, the mandala and other transcendental symbols. Words — symbols of meaning — and especially words in their most symbolic arrangements, that is, poetry — were a potent avenue of exploration for a new kind of crossover art. This crossover took place in the sides of the brain, so that even how to experience a work of art, or even tell what kind of art it was, was no longer obvious.

In fact, it was two crossover arts, meeting in the middle: the visual arts, and literature. The junction of the two is already axiomatic, of course, because the written word *is*, by definition, a visible, designed thing. This show traces the practice that began in the mid-20th century of using visual form to augment, break down or replace the meanings represented within the symbols we call words, and they're more concerned with this process than with how pretty it is.

Typography is sexy these days. Whole studies exist on the lettering found on buildings, for example, and the cult font, Helvetica — which was of course designed in that fecund decade, the 50s — even has a cult feature film about it. (Douglas Coupland wrote of Helvetica, 'The font is a rock star.') As long as writing has existed, its form has been important. But in some of the work on display here the form of type is the least interesting thing going on. Liliane Lijn's cones, for example, use letraset.

She wrote in 1968: 'WORDS = VIBRATIONS = ENERGY,' and her cones put that idea into literal practice. Dom Sylvester Houédard and Christopher Knowles used typewriter letters to form shapes and patterns on paper, making a virtue of the linearity of the medium; in some pieces the patterns created by the back-and-forth of the typewriter arm resemble Navajo weavings. With sentences broken down to words, which have no meaning beyond their appearance — and words broken down to letters — shapes yield fragments of meaning, like a race memory. Spin the cone and even that disappears into the particular abstract Energy of the particle.

The presiding spirit of the exhibition is the Scottish writer and artist Ian Hamilton Finlay, whose magazine *Poor. Old. Tired. Horse* was a leading vehicle of concrete poetry in the UK in the 50s and 60s. Finlay later repudiated the movement — for being too popular — and moved over to sculpture, creating his astonishing garden Little Sparta, outside Edinburgh, with poems carved into rocks. The concrete, conceptual and picture poems on display in issues of *Poor. Old. Tired. Horse* toy with graphics and meaning. Letters sink into other letters to make new combinations and visual puns; repetitions of words with one letter missing or different show up possibilities of interpretation. Finlay's rather Spartan rigour encompasses a definite playfulness, which is very infectious.

There is an intense charm to this work, glossed with nostalgia for the best of the 50s and 60s: the real artistic liberation and experimentation, about fun. A large drawing — I mean poem — of a ship (by Finlay and John Furnival) with the title *A History of English Taste for 1797, R George III* applies to poetry the permissions won for visual art by the Dada pioneers of nearly 100 years ago: 'It's a poem if you say it is.'

That this world of childlike discovery had a sell-by date is evident moving into the 70s and beyond, where forms were already becoming more rigid and the jokes fewer. Liliane Lijn's cones, mentioned earlier, carry this spirit through, and her new work — not featured here — uses rods of light to, well, luminous effect.

For example, one surprise in the exhibition, dating from

1975, is a series of typescripts by the minimalist artist Carl André, more famous for his famous 'pile of bricks' in the Tate. Framed on one wall are five pages of a 17-page poem called Shooting the Script. Using small blocks of words in truncated form, repeated, cut off, arranged in a sort of grid on the page, the 'poem' creates a prism effect around a real-life shooting that took place in Texas in 1898. The work echoes his later sculptural work visually, with its rigid arrangement of blocks of words on the page. It makes a demand to be approached as a work of visual art as well as through the meaning of language. And with its rather filmic cuts and repeats with small changes, it is also the first work within this exhibition to explore the conditions of narrative.

This is less gimmicky, more complex and — strangely — more about the materials (in this case, words) than André's more 'material' sculptures; it's one of the most surprising and interesting works in the exhibition. The poem's wit and evident purity of purpose is only slightly undermined by the way the artist signed each sheet: '©carl andré ©1975'.

The sixties and seventies also produced traditional work alongisde the dismantling being done by the concrete poets and conceptual artists. Illustrative work by Robert Smithson, Alasdair Gray and Philippe Guston/Clark Coolidge looks less transgressive (though at the time, Guston was driven out of New York by the scathing reactions of critics when he abandoned abstract painting) but carries on various strands of enquiry.

Guston's cartoonish drawings have a Crumb-like feel and naïf handwritten text. Gray's work is more Baroque, with stylised iconographic images arranged around gorgeously calligraphed poems. These poems, relying on the full panoply of prosody and syntax, come as a surprise after the atomisation of meaning in the previous rooms. In fact, it is interesting to note the extent to which the viewer has to disengage with the visual look of the poems in order to read them as poems — which they demand. They invoke that other great poet-engraver, Blake, whose ghost is also present in two very different drawings by Robert Smithson. In the delicate lines of the 50s and early 60s (think of Warhol's commercial art), his doodles become architectural, curlicues turn out to be Os or loops of repeated letters, and his archetypal nudes look like Blake's angels.

Hockney's drawings are also familiar, being his illustrations for Cafavy's poems about homosexual life in 1920s Alexandria. They feature no text, so their only raison d'être is that they were conceived as illustrations for one. But that text is nowhere on display here.

The exhibition ends with a room of contemporary pieces by younger artists, which raise some interesting ideas but all in all seem less adventurous than what those pioneers of half a century ago were producing — especially when you consider the technological and social changes since then. Pieces here seem to have been chosen for their similarity to the earlier work, or because they are like one another, rather than because they push the boundaries of language and visual meaning now.

With a couple of exceptions — like Sue Tompkins, whose disjointed typed phrases echo both the typewriter images and the language-breakdown concrete poetry of the earlier rooms — the younger artists seem to view words more as graphic. That is, they explore the expressiveness of type itself, and the interaction of type and pictorial elements. Maybe this is the inevitable result of the commercialisation of art, alongside the respectability commercial art now enjoys as a genre (there is nothing wrong with that; only that less commercial work is then further marginalised, and this is also happening in mainstream poetry and fiction). In two works by Los Angeles artist Frances Stark the text forms a field or background, with which a figure either interacts or simply coexists. Matthew Brannon's

Words on a Page features a graphical typewriter and coffee cup, with text above in a typewriter font. Unlike in Stark's pieces there is no interaction; the words and the machine exist together as a rather pleasant, but ultimately unchallenging, picture.

Janice Kerbel's giant circus-inspired posters, on the other hand, use an instantly recognisable visual trope to create a way for her strange, dreamy visions to operate. Iggy Fatuse and Faintgirl perform daring feats in the lyrical poetic language, the circus of a dream. They take off precisely because the typographical poster's graphic problems — text size, emphasis, and also cultural connotations — create a structural frame for the 'action'. They are much simpler than the old posters, in strong black on a clean white ground, and intensely beautiful.

Sue Tompkins and Karl Holmqvist are the two most poetry-based contemporary artists on display here, and both of them rely on performance and sound as well as visual effect. Tompkins' work is the most purely poetic, as opposed to visual, on display, and while the accompanying magazine describes her as more of a 'rebellious offspring' than a 'clear descendant' of the old concrete poets, this work doesn't seem to stretch their discoveries very far.

By pure chance, an article in the current issue of *Poetry* magazine (founded in Chicago in 1912 and now part of the Poetry Foundation) exposes some of the shortfall of this exhibition. Kenneth Goldsmith, in 'Flarf is Dionysus; Conceptual Writing is Apollo', writes:

Why atomize, shatter, and splay language into nonsensical shards when you can hoard, store, mold, squeeze, shovel, soil, scrub, package, and cram the stuff into towers of words and castles of language with a stroke of the keyboard? And what fun to wreck it: knock it down, hit delete, and start all over again. There's a sense of gluttony, of joy, and of fun. Like kids at a touch table, we're delighted to feel language again, to roll in it, to get our hands dirty. With so much available language, does anyone really need to write more? Instead, let's just process what exists. Language as matter; language as material. How much did you say that paragraph weighed?

Poems published as examples include the comic-strip panels of Gary Sullivan's 'Am I Emo?', numerous Flarf and conceptual poems, and the image poem *The Great Order of the Universe* by the experimental Canadian poet Christian Bök. This piece, with its tightly integrated use of visual and verbal elements, and the fact that neither can be understood at all without the other, is a far more sophisticated exploration of language, what we see and how meaning operates than most of the contemporary part of the ICA show. Bök creates a visual grammar.

Like the best work elsewhere in the exhibition he offers us a chance to examine how a poem — as opposed to a picture — works in the brain, how a visual artwork operates in it, and how (or if!) we want these experiences to be differentiated.

Two other younger artists I've come across lately, whose work addresses these themes, are May Cornet, based in England but with a French father, and the French artist Delphine Vincent.

In *I Can't Stand the Rain* Cornet uses newsprint to express the dolour of rain, putting the words that are incidentally on it at one remove, and strangely intensifying the sadness. This is reminiscent of those mid-century artists downstairs — with a bit of Schwitters showing through — working on the quiet, suggesting meaning. Collage is itself like a visual form of 'found poetry', and the printed words on collage elements were a very important part of that throughout the 20th century.

Cornet's 'o drawings' are meticulous and strangely moving abstracts made of endless repetition of the letter o, presenting it as molecules within sweeping, suggestive waves, or else as a meditation. They are evocative of the games we used to play as children, saying one word over and over till it has no meaning any more, and I thought of them the instant I saw Smithson's delicate, childlike loops of nearly 50 years ago.

Likewise, Delphine Vincent's canvases introduce a hugely important element that is almost entirely missing from this show: colour. It is very common among people with synaesthesia, for example, including myself, to see letters – or numbers – in specific colours. In fact, I used to see words in white trailing across the top of my (black) mind's eye. This phenomenon is alluded to in Douglas Coupland's article 'Visual Thinking', reprinted in the current issue of *Roland*, the magazine of the ICA's visual arts programme, which accompanies this exhibition:

> Here's another question I was recently asked: when I see words in my mind, what font aew they in? The answer: Helvetica. It's a strange question, but you know what I'm getting at: how do you see actual words in your head as you think? Or do you see words at all? Is it a voice in your head? Do you see subtitles?

This talk of multi-sensory experience corresponds to the well-documented fact that many composers 'see' music in colours. (And I once overheard a pontificating gallery-goer explaining to his companions how, using the colours and shapes as a guide, one could 'read' the music in a Kandinsky painting: 'that bit there', for example, being a B flat, et cetera.) Take this primary link to the creativity of practitioners, add the prevalence of colour in contemporary graphic design (say), and it is easy to see how important colour is in how we experience language.

Vincent's work consists of canvases with a phrase, often taken from pop culture, in raised letters. The letters are in a plain,

Helvetica-like font, and the whole thing is painted in one colour. Her colours are bold, vibrant and subtle, and the meaning of the phrases is emphasised, distorted and brought into focus — almost as an interrogation — by the way they sink onto the surface or rise from it according to the light. This work is deceptively simple — the artist says she seeks 'la beauté du verbe' — and, like Ian Hamilton Finlay's explorations fifty years ago, it uses this perfectly realised simplicity to isolate and expose meanings within a visual vocabulary of surprise. Beauty.

The visual sense — the moving image, graphics, design, the paparazzo shot, the nonlinearity of the web page — is becoming entrenched now as almost our society's primary way of transmitting information. Some might say the text is dead, but there is so much contemporary work, both art and poetry, joining the two together that it feels like an important avenue to look at closely. It's about how things looks, but it's also about what we think meaning is.

Ian Hamilton Finlay wrote: 'Stupidity reduces language to words. This exhibition could embody a chiasmic reversal of that statement: 'Stupidity reduces words to language.' And freedom is both visual and verbal.

BY THE LIGHT OF THE SILVERY MOON
DOWSON, SCHOENBERG AND THE BIRTH OF MODERNISM

'The death of Ernest Dowson will mean very little to the world at large, but it will mean a great deal to the few people who care passionately for poetry', wrote Arthur Symonds in 1900. 'A little book of verses, the manuscript of another, a one-act play in verse... some translations from the French, done for money; that is all that was left by a man who was undoubtedly a man of genius, not a great poet, but a poet, one of the very few writers of our generation to whom that name can be applied in its most intimate sense.'

The subject came up on a walk, one rainy Sunday last year, in south London's Brockley Cemetery. My companion and I were standing at Ernest Dowson's grave, at the very spot where Symons himself may have stood with head bowed. We had arrived to find it, though heavily vandalised, literally garlanded in laurels, with a half-full bottle of absinthe nestled among the leaves. As we strolled away from the grave, the question was this: 'Who, as in which poets, would you defend, if it came to it, in an argument?'

My answer seemed to be Dowson. He certainly isn't a major poet, and much of what he wrote isn't even very good. But posterity has seen to that side of the argument, so I chose to defend him. He is not at all without charm, either: a kind of charm that Keats and, for example, Isaac Rosenberg had — the charm of being a genuine, striving, earnest — and doomed — young person. There is a localised, London charm, too: these three were all highly indigenous to London. And Dowson also has a strange recurring reach into unlikely areas (one of his poems even features at the end of the noir film Laura). He is one of those people who simply crop up.

Ernest Dowson — the ultimate aesthete, equally addicted to prostitutes and (sentimentally) little girls, lilies and absinthe — died, aged 32, in a friend's lodgings in Catford, of either (depending on which view you take) tuberculosis or alcoholism. Even aside from the fact that he was dying, his situation was desperate. Following that discussion a year ago, this is the story of how he came to play a bit part in the formation of one of the most Modern of all the Modernist projects of the 20th century: the atonal music of Arnold Schoenberg.

Two deaths, both tragic and both marked with the period, bookend that year and mark the irrevocable close of the Decadent nineties. The first was Ernest Dowson's, on 23 February; the second, on 30 November, was Oscar Wilde's. The seal was set on the epoch only two months later, when Queen Victoria herself joined them on 22 January 1901.

But the world of poetry — at least, the world of poetry that got read and noticed, at least in English — would remain much as it had been for several years yet. The touch paper wouldn't go up — wouldn't 'lick its tongue into the corners of the evening' — for another 15 years. Just as we're told sex was invented in 1963, poetic Modernism apocryphally was born caterwauling with the publication of *The Love Song of J Alfred Prufrock*.

But the paper had been lit before that. In fact, the paper is always getting lit. A series of random events made 1909, our own year's pre-centenary, a cluster year towards the new century's aesthetic. But as the arrow began to point forward, like the hands of Dorothy's Scarecrow it was also pointing back, far into the 19th century. Because nothing is ever just beginning. You can chuck out your chintz, but you can't chuck out everybody else's. And arguably you can't chuck out yours either. You have to wait till it wears out.

We're taught about Art or Music or Poetry (if we're lucky) as if 'this' period gave way to 'that' school, which forced 'this' breakaway group to write 'that' manifesto. It's as if everybody alive went to the Salon d'Automne and mocked the blinkered critics. It's neat, it's tidy, it's unchallenging, it makes *us* look good (if you subscribe to the idea of progress), and it turns *1066 and All That* into a workable educationalist template. In this way, from a very early age, we are encouraged not to look at things, or wonder about them; just assign them a year and away we go, to our studio in happening Hoxton.

The reality, of course, is that if you walked into a house at random, you wouldn't see a house full of things that 'date from' this year. You'd see the furniture, books, curtain fabric from the last 10, 30, 90 years. You'd see your trendy mate poring over the latest issue of *Wallpaper** curled up in the chair his mother bought when he was ten (though he probably wouldn't still have her black velvet clown painting unless he was called Wayne Hemingway.) The revolutionaries may have new stuff, but they also still have their chintz — it's precisely what they can't even see, they're so used to it. They have it because it's comfy and someone gave it to them.

The 1900s were the years of Picasso's blue and rose periods. *Les Demoiselles D'Avignon*'s aggressive primitivism pretty much put paid to the late Victorian discovery of Orientalism, which of course flourished on in high Art Nouveau style (though it would never quite replace it as a basis for home furnishings). The decade saw Richard Strauss' shocking opera Salomé (based on Wilde's shocking play) and the first stirrings of Gertrude Stein. (For unlikely pairings and era-overlap, consider the interesting fact that, when young, Gertrude Stein looked strikingly like Beatrix Potter.) Levels of dissonance in music had been steadily rising since the late-19th century. Liszt's *Bagatelle Sans Tonalité* was written in 1885 (three years after Wilde's embarrassing trip to America as a specimen Aesthetic, in the pay of D'Oyly Carte — during which he found opportunity to make Henry James feel provincial), Debussy swirled the colours around like paints in a pot in the nineties, and Satie the 'phonometrician' wrote his strange, light, off-kilter pieces alongside.

Poetry, however, was different: in English, the 1900s were the years of Thomas Hardy, Alfred Noyes, Yeats, Robert Service, Walter De La Mare. 1905, mopping up the puddles of the nineties, saw the publication of Ernest Dowson's *Collected Poems* as well as Symond's *A Book of Twenty Songs* — and Wilde's posthumous essay about his incarceration, *De Profundis*. There was a small offering from the young James Joyce halfway through the decade, and one from Stein. But in 1907 that arch-conservative bugbear, Kipling, was awarded the Nobel Prize for Literature. Ten years after Debussy's *Prélude à l'Après-Midi d'un Faune* (itself based on Mallarmé's great Symbolist poem of 1876), poetry audiences — still large at that point — were reading new collections by Swinburne, Hardy and Henry Newbolt.

Then something happened. On December 21, 1908, a concert audience in Vienna sat down to hear Arnold Schoenberg's String Quartet No. 2. It was a musical sensation; the composers were more forward-thinking than the poets at this stage, but the public was finding their worst excesses hard to handle. To say Schoenberg had had a bad year would be an understatement: only that autumn he had discovered that his wife Mathilde was having an affair with a young Expressionist painter, Richard Gerstl. When Mathilde broke it off, Gerstl had retaliated by staging a spectacular, possibly too Expressionist, suicide. After this episode apparently there was nowhere left, musically, for Schoenberg's state of mind to go. The string quartet he had been working on all autumn became a lesson in evocative disintegration — an orgy of atonal uncertainty and despair, punctuated and heightened by a ghostly floating hint of a nursery tune (*Ach, Du Lieber Augustin*; in English, *Did You Ever See a Lassie?*), and partly set to words, and with no anchoring key signature, melody or pretty effect to cling to. It ended in chaos, with hisses and jeers from a crowd that had already been expecting the worst — some of them even had noisemakers with them, just in case. In the weeks that followed it was written about everywhere as 'the Schoenberg affair'.

The two wordy movements in that Quartet are set to poems from *Der Siebente Ring* (*The Seventh Ring*), by the German Symbolist poet and translator Stefan George, who was crucial to Schoenberg's oeuvre. They are deeply indicative of Schoenberg's state of mind at the time:

> Deep is the sadness that gloomily comes over me,
> Again I step, Lord, in your house.
> Long was the ride, my limbs are weary,
> The shrines are empty, only anguish is full.
> ...
> Kill the longing, close the wound!
> Take my love away, give me your joy.

The next month, in London, the cocky 25-year-old poet TE Hulme (who would be blown up in the trenches in 1917, along with the only manuscript of his important monograph on Jacob Epstein) published the first poems that could arguably be called Imagist. He then seceded from the Poets' Club, of which he was secretary, to form a breakaway group which he imaginatively called the Secession Club.

In April 1909 a young American poet called Ezra Pound was invited to join Hulme's group, and the 20th century was in business. It wasn't before time, either: as late as 1908 Pound had seen fit to title his second collection *A Quinzane for This Yule*. Here is an extract from

Aube of the West Dawn, Venetian June:

> Then svelte the dawn reflected in the west,
> As did the sky slip off her robes of night,
> I see to stand mine armouress confessed,
> Then doth my spirit know himself aright,
> And tremulous against her faint-flushed breast
> Doth cast him quivering, her bondsman quite.

The Secession Club set to work stripping away the varnish (what Alan Bennett's fictitious Kafka, in 'The Insurance Man', would call 'the sheer weight of Prague') — writing light, shimmering poems based on principles of simplicity, clarity and — well — images. The first Imagist anthology was out that year in time for Christmas.

1909 was the year Picasso painted the first work of Analytical Cubism, the *Portrait of Ambroise Vollard*. Schoenberg's student Anton Webern wrote his *Six Pieces for Orchestra*. Algernon Charles Swinburne, the hyper-Victorian flagellist and versifier, perished.

It was the year in which Arthur Symonds had a psychotic breakdown that would remove him more or less permanently from the literary scene. (It's hard to imagine, but Symonds lived on until 1945, writing nothing of any note, stuck in his time; in the 1930s John Betjeman wrote a tragic poem — in the head waiter's book — about seeing the old Decadent sitting, alone and pathetic, in the Café Royal:

> I saw him in the Café Royal
> Very old and very grand.
> Modernistic shone the lamplight
> There in London's fairyland...)

In the summer of 1909, still deranged from the cataclysm of the previous autumn, Schoenberg wrote: 'I have only one hope — that I will not live much longer'. He wrote, 'in a word — I am totally broken'.

In *The Rest is Noise*, his survey of 20th century music, Alex Ross writes that Schoenberg 'warned that he would "soon follow the path, find the resolution, that at long last might be the highest culmination of human actions"'. But, in an intriguingly vague turn of phrase, he could not foresee 'whether it will be my body that will give way or my soul'. One might even say, in a gothically Decadent turn of phrase.

Ross reports that during this time he also wrote, to Kandinsky: 'Art belongs to the unconscious! One must express oneself! Express oneself *directly*! Not one's taste, or one's upbringing, or one's intelligence, knowledge or skill'. He told Alma Mahler to listen for 'colours, noises, lights, sounds, movements, glances, gestures'.

Cut to a dark and stormy might. It was 1913. Although it would never prove possible to wean him off the Orientals, Pound was finally about to achieve the famous two-line apogee of Imagism, his *In a Station of the Metro*:

The apparition of these faces in the crowd;
Petals on a wet, black bough.

Schoenberg had weathered his near-breakdown, and the intervening years proved a colourful hardening. He had discovered in the aftermath of Gerstl's suicide the beginning of his true path, and knew he had to take modern music beyond tonality. Beyond what he might have considered his early Late Romantic pandering, and into the world of strange structures. (Schoenberg, already an angry man, was made even angrier by the common term used to describe his music. 'To call any relation of tones atonal', he wrote, 'is just as farfetched as it would be to designate a relation of colors aspectral or acomplementary. There is no such antithesis'. He wrote, again related by Ross: 'I find above all that the expression "atonal music" is most unfortunate — it is on a par with calling flying "the art of not falling", or swimming "the art of not drowning". Only in the language of publicity is it thought adequate to emphasize in this way a negative quality of whatever is being advertised'.

Always keen to make his point, Schoenberg went on to state that:

'... this expression is wrong: with tones only what is tonal, in keeping with the nature of tones, can be produced; there must at least be that connection of tones based on the tonal, which has to exist between any two tones if they are to form a progression that is at all logical and comprehensible; an opposite, "atonal" can no more exist among tones and tone-relationships than can an opposite "aspectral" or "acomplementary", among colours and progressions of colours'.)

And because any vestige of tunefulness was seen as a betrayal of this hard new sense, in the way that rhyme (say) has subsequently come to be considered old hat, it was necessary to find new structures to support these pieces. For this reason, even the most abstract artists in the most abstract century's most abstract art form continued to work with lyrics, making something as cosy-sounding as *songs*. Schoenberg was no exception.

Some of the lyrics Schoenberg worked to (for his *Erwartung, Pierrot Lunaire, Die Glückliche Hand*) were written by amateur poets — including himself — and were as Expressionist as the music he set them to. But he found other inspirations, in a darker, older Symbolism.

Schoenberg was particularly attracted to the work of Stefan George — whose work, as Alex Ross says in *The Rest is Noise*, 'showed

Schoenberg a way out of the easygoing pleasures of Viennese aesthetics. The sheer density of the poet's imagery did not permit easy access, although sensual secrets resided in the labyrinth'. The labyrinth, needless to say, was where Ernest Dowson also lived.

Dowson was even more the consummate Decadent than his friend Symonds. He was so addicted to ethereal beauty that he didn't even have a proper home. He calculated that a prostitute was cheaper than a hotel, identified at least as much with France as with England (Wikipedia calls him 'a kind of English Verlaine'), and existed on absinthe and lilies and food from the cabmen's shelters. He invented the witticism, 'absinthe makes the tart grow fonder'. He was devoted for most of his adult life (not very long, remember) to a Polish waitress called Adelaide, who was 11 when he started frequenting her parents' café. He was a legendary, and quite scary, bon viveur and drunk. Both his parents had killed themselves; he was literally waiting for his ship to come in, in the form of some compensation for the failure of the defunct family dockyard in Limehouse. And he knew absolutely everybody, including the King of the Decadents, Oscar Wilde.

In short, Dowson was the symptom of the disease, of the reason Modernism had to happen, in a nutshell: the living embodiment of the apogee of the decay of Victorian sentimental ornamentism. So says an acquaintance, an intelligent, discerning, unsentimental man, who tried to read Dowson's poems in a slim volume bound in red calf, and ended up throwing it across the room. His complaint was anticipated by more than a century (things were beginning to change, after all, even in 1900) by Symons, who continues:

'People will complain, probably, in his verses, of what will seem to them the factitious melancholy, the factitious idealism, and (peeping through at a few rare moments) the factitious suggestions of riot. They will see only a literary affectation, where in truth there is as genuine a note of personal sincerity as in the more explicit and arranged confessions of less admirable poets'.

Symons goes on to articulate the thing that makes Dowson's rather florid poetry live, which I also articulated to my questioning friend: it's just that he seems, like Pinocchio, to be a Real Boy. Here is Symons again:

> 'To Dowson, as to all those who have not been 'content to ask unlikely gifts in vain,' nature, life, destiny, whatever one chooses to call it, that power which is strength to the strong, presented itself as a barrier against which all one's strength only served to dash one to more hopeless ruin. He was not a dreamer; destiny passes by the dreamer, sparing him because he clamours for nothing. He was a child, clamouring for so many things, all impossible. With a body too weak for ordinary existence, he desired all the enchantments of all the senses. With a soul too shy to tell its own secret, except in exquisite evasions, he desired the boundless confidence of love'.

Before we go on, here are some Dowson stanzas, which may (as Thurber might have put it) refresh your memory. First, from his zappily-titled *Non Sum Qualis Eram Bonae Sub Regno Cynarae*:

> I have forgot much, Cynara! gone with the wind,
> Flung roses, roses riotously with the throng,
> Dancing, to put thy pale, lost lilies out of mind;
> But I was desolate and sick of an old passion,
> Yea, all the time, because the dance was long:
> I have been faithful to thee, Cynara! in my fashion.

And second, from his *Vitae Summa Brevis*:

They are not long, the days of wine and roses:
Out of a misty dream
Our path emerges for a while, then closes
Within a dream.

Notice anything familiar in there? Have you, in the recesses of your consciousness, started saying to yourself, 'Frankly my dear, I don't give a damn!'? Or humming show tunes from *Kiss Me Kate*?

But that's not all. Not only did Dowson insert three figurative phrases straight into the heart of our colloquial language — which is more than a lot of poets have managed — he is also the first person recorded in the English language to have used the word 'soccer'. And what is nearly as little known as this is that his High Victorian words were also (in the German translation of Stefan George) used as the basis for a song by no less titanically Modernist a master than the future 12-tone guru himself, our other hero, Arnold Schoenberg.

On this occasion, as he peered through his famous spectacles at a sheaf of translations, a poem called *Seraphita* caught Schoenberg's eye. He was already interested in making some form of music drama after another *Seraphita* — the 1835 novel of another distinctly pre-Modernist writer, Balzac. Here is what he read, in Dowson's original English:

Come not before me now, O visionary face!
Me tempest-tost, and borne along life's passionate sea;
Troublous and dark and stormy though my passage be;
Not here and now may we commingle or embrace,
Lest the loud anguish of the waters should efface
The bright illumination of thy memory,
Which dominates the night; rest, far away from me,
In the serenity of thine abiding-place!
But when the storm is highest, and the thunders blare,

And sea and sky are riven, O moon of all my night!
Stoop down but once in pity of my great despair,
And let thine hand, though over late to help, alight
But once upon my pale eyes and my drowning hair,
Before the great waves conquer in the last vain fight.

With three shorter pieces by Rilke he set a German translation of this poem to music, creating his important atonal song sequence, the fetchingly titled Opus 22.

There is a huge seam of moon-lore in Decadent and symbolist literature — far more than there is in Modernist literature. This extends to a whole seam of Pierrot imagery. Just confining ourselves to the artists already under discussion, Wilde uses the moon as a major symbol in his *Salomé*, where the moon's face changes to signify the emotional content of the action — which ends with Salomé's murder by Herod:

THE PAGE OF HERODIAS
Look at the moon. How strange the moon seems! She is like a woman rising from a tomb. She is like a dead woman. One might fancy she was looking for dead things.

THE YOUNG SYRIAN
She has a strange look. She is like a little princess who wears a yellow veil, and whose feet are of silver. She is like a princess who has little white doves for feet. One might fancy she was dancing.

THE PAGE OF HERODIAS
She is like a woman who is dead. She moves very slowly.

Wilde's *Salomé*, considered too shocking for London, had its first performance in 1896 in Paris. Wilde was in prison, but Ernest Dowson attended the play with Aubrey Beardsley. Strauss' opera, based on Wilde's play, opened to scandalised crowds in Dresden in 1905.

And of course Schoenberg's own *Pierrot Lunaire*, using poems by the French poet Albert Giraud (translated into German by Eric Harleben, who used to recite or chant them in music halls and cabarets), celebrates this same aesthetic in very jarring Sprechstimme vocals that are much harder to listen to, even a hundred years later, than the lyric is to read. (I have heard an eyewitness report of paying customers walking out of it in the Barbican in 2009.) Here, translated into English by Cecil Gray, is a small sample:

> The pallid buds of moonlight
> Those pale and wondrous roses
> Bloom in the nights of summer—
> O could I pluck but one!
> ...
> As a lingering drop of blood
> Stains the lip of a consumptive,
> So this music is pervaded
> By a morbid deathly charm.

In other words: the music was so far ahead of its time as to be *still* ahead of its time, and the lyric was, frankly, in a manner that any gothy adolescent can relate to. Except that they would have called it Romantic back then, instead of Emo. In 1897, Dowson had also written a moon-drunk one-act play, *The Pierrot of the Minute*, about a Pierrot who is allowed to fall in love for one night with a moon-nymph, on the firm understanding that it will ruin his life:

> THE LADY (reads)
> "Au Petit Trianon, at night's full noon,
> Mortal, beware the kisses of the moon!

Whoso seeks her she gathers like a flower —
He gives a life, and only gains an hour."

PIERROT (laughing recklessly)
Bear me away to thine enchanted bower,
All of my life I venture for an hour.

Beardsley, who illustrated it (and would be dead of TB at 25), called it a 'foolish little playlet'; but then, he also insulted Wilde's play, which he most famously illustrated. (Wilde, in his turn, disliked the pictures.) *Pierrot of the Minute* is quite revealing, in an incidental way, of Dowson's biographical proclivities: the moon is as symbolically pale, unattainable and asexual as a little girl, and the doomed life the Pierrot is destined to lead afterwards is foretold.

Dowson's *Seraphita* makes the longest song in Opus 22. Schoenberg's decision to set Brockley's distinguished deceased to music has been criticised for being a throwback to a less-developed taste; but on the contrary, as we can see, the poem was still in 1913 — just about — au courant; and its inward-looking, rather maudlin text suits Schoenberg's music, which was still at that stage, overtly emotional. And finally, there are senses in which the Moonlight Pierrot could simply be read as another version of the eternally popular sexy, hungry vampire hero.

'It doesn't make Dowson any better a poet'. This is the voice of David Secombe, my Brockley walking companion and author of *I Have Been Faithful to Thee, Ernest! In My Fashion* — a tragic-farcical play about Dowson and the nature of failure. 'But it goes to show that rigid definitions like 'Victorian', 'decadent', 'symbolist', 'expressionist' and 'modernist' can be misleading. The common aesthetic preoccupations of the late Victorian and Edwardian world were strong enough to mitigate against easy classification'.

It's all a long way from the generation of poets then working their way up: the bankers, doctors, insurance men, publishers, staid men of letters who kept their expressionist tendencies well-wrapped and sought to eliminate, as TS Eliot abjured us to do, the personality from his art (with, we might say, mixed success). At this stage the great Modernist composer Charles Ives ('a great man', according to Schoenberg) was breaking the sound barrier all by himself in secret, at weekends, in between transforming the fledgling American discipline of selling life insurance.

Back in Brockley Cemetery, where the whole top of Dowson's cross had been knocked off, we found a plastic document wallet nestled among the garland of laurel. Some very faded, large, bold, italic lines of poetry were printed on pink paper inside it — evidence of some local school project on the local literary heritage, maybe. (We took it off, naturally, for the picture, but put it back afterwards.) Were all these artefacts connected? Had the apocryphal pupils really worked out such a deep understanding of what Ernest would like best? Did the teacher really tell them about the Green Fairy and the death in Catford? One imagines that they weren't played any Schoenberg music. I like to think that if it *was* the kids who left the absinthe they at least got their teacher to buy it for them.

Literary criticism, like history, is the story of the victors. If Dowson was a Victorian, so was Schoenberg: he was 25 when Dowson died at 32. He lasted until 1951, dying in distant Beverley Hills, prophet and scourge into the ages of the machine, Bauhaus, the New Look, almost the atomic fifties. Eisenhower would be elected two years later. Poor Ernest only reached Catford, and never saw a telephone or a movie. What would he have written if he'd lived to develop his art past the little green-lit window allotted to him?

Dowson, like Schoenberg, like Keats before them, died thinking he was misunderstood and a failure. He wanted his aesthetic to prevail, but he also wanted popular success. Like all writers and artists, he wanted to be loved — on his own terms, for his art. Little did he know that he would influence and inspire both the godfather of the highbrow, and the as-yet-unimaginable populist, Cole Porter — in that future world so many artists would escape into. Had he lived even another nine years, to the edge of the century that still touches us, he might have come out of the Café Royal one night whistling a new song, a hundred years old in the year this article was first published:

> By the light, of the silvery moon,
> I want to spoon,
> To my honey I'll croon love's tune.
> Honey moon, keep a-shinin' in June.
> Your silv'ry beams will bring love's dreams,
> We'll be cuddlin' soon,
> By the silvery moon.

NOW I'M A REAL BOY
POETRY'S PLAGIARISM PROBLEM

In March this year, a woman went to the launch of *Laventville*, the second collection by Sheree Mack, a Newcastle poet with a massive Facebook friends list and a strong local poetry coterie. Having bought the book (which presumably means that Mack signed it for her), Imagine her surprise when, reading it, she found one of her own poems loosely copied inside it.

Plagiarism used to be something those sort of guys who would describe themselves as 'net-savvy' would talk about, showing up in writing workshops with a © before their names on their manuscripts, assuring you that it asserted 'ownership' over their work, and that now no one could 'steal their idea'.

How I used to laugh.

But fast-forward 20 years or so, and most poets won't forget the names such as Christian Ward, Graham Nunn, or CJ Allen in a hurry. It seems there are people who really do want to steal your idea. No one knows why. Now Sheree Mack has taken the thing to a new level, and redefined what 'plagiarism' actually means. The poetry world is riven.

The art form's recent plagiarism cases have been meticulously investigated by Ira Lightman, the UK's prodigiously gifted 'poetry sleuth', who has worked tirelessly to set the record straight, to find the copied poems and restore them, as it were, to their rightful owners. He's been accused of witch-hunting, a charge he vehemently denies. In the Mack case, the aforementioned woman spent two months of emailing back and forth with both Sheree Mack and her publisher

(Andy Croft at Smokestack Books, a very well-respected northern poetry press), before she gave up and went to Ira Lightman, much as one might go to Sherlock Holmes. Mack had admitted copying two poems. Lightman reports: 'The publisher seemed to have made no effort at all to check the other poems in *Laventille*. I found a dozen more examples in about two hours.' He then found more. And more.

Every time the debate varies; each plagiarist (like each unhappy family) is a little different from the others. The case of the Australian Graham Nunn, accused of lifting lines from Canadian Don McKay, provoked storms of debate about the ethics of 'found' poetry, and postmodern writing techniques, and the contemporary culture of poems 'after' somebody else.

John Ashbery once wrote a cento — an ancient Roman form where each line is taken from a different poem — thinking he had invented the form. The former poet laureate himself, Andrew Motion, got into a bit of trouble with some unattributed quotes. Everybody's doing it.

Reactions to Lightman's revelations have been mixed. There are two camps ranged against each other. One is the 'pitchforks at dawn' set, unable to get over their outraged assertions about how borrowing some words just the same as stealing Grandma's silver; and the other is formed of those who feel sorry for the thief, and feel that Grandma's silver had a kind of open-source feel about it, anyway.

The poets Mack had copied from included the well-known US poet August Kleinzahler, published in the UK by Faber. He responded saying that his solicitor would be in touch with Smokestack.

They included Douglas Dunn, whose signature poem of taciturn miners — 'Men of Terry Street', set in the northeast of

England — Mack transplanted to Trinidad with strange palimpsest-style changes that make no sense. In Dunn, 'This masculine invisibility makes gods of them'; in Mack, it only makes 'good' of them. Dunn's 'pantheon of boots and overalls' becomes 'a phantom of bare feet and string vests'. And where Dunn's grim-faced heroic providers 'hold up their children and sing to them', Mack's 'hold their children at arms-length and chastise'. Her version of the poem finishes with a signature mark, a sentimental line that sums up what she's trying to say. The poem falls flat, the heroism of Dunn's miners becomes merely kvetching.

Throughout 2014, the canal poet laureate Jo Bell had been running a wildly successful weekly poetry-prompt website called 52, and an associated Facebook group where members could share their resulting poems. The group had 500 members, and many of them were posting poems up every week in the very-much-closed group. As of 21 May, Bell had discovered three poems Sheree Mack had copied from 52; by now there may be more.

Perhaps predictably, Mack seems to have copied one poem from Jo Bell herself — who would, had things been different, have been sharing a stage with her opening this year's Ledbury Poetry Festival.

Before the controversy, Smokestack described *Laventille* on its website as: '[T]he forgotten story of the 1970 Black Power Revolution in Trinidad and Tobago, when for forty-five days an uprising of students, trade unions and the disaffected poor threatened to overthrow the government. The book is a 'shrine of remembrances' for the ordinary people behind the headlines.'

There is an authenticity being claimed here. Sadly — very sadly — it seems not to be genuine. Kei Miller, a Jamaican poet based in the UK, wrote a long and thoughtful blog post about the debacle. He refers to Dunn's poem, saying:

...to my mind, Mack's book belongs squarely in this debate about Caribbean authenticity. A number of factors have shielded her from it so far: most obviously, her book was out for too short a time for it to register amongst many Caribbean readers and it has subsequently been withdrawn and pulped (though with a promise that it will be reissued in 2016); it was published by a press that doesn't give ready access to a Caribbean market; and thirdly, the fact of race undoubtedly gives Mack an added layer of insulation from what one of my friends calls the 'blacklash'. Had Mack's collection been out for a longer time, and had it reached to *Laventille* and the rest of the Caribbean, and had it been published by a press such as Peepal Tree, and had she been racialized as anything other than black, I suspect she would have found herself in the middle of a whole other storm.

Though born and raised in England, Sheree Mack does have some claim to the Caribbean through parents. I believe she has family in Laventille — the eponymous community of her controversial book. But it is interesting that when she tries to evoke Laventille she has to use the template of other poems set in other places.

The one thing no one really knows about these plagiarists is this: why do they do it? It seems to me obvious that this is self-harming activity; surely, every time a plagiarist publishes a poem and all their friends compliment them on it, it just confirms them in their own conviction that a poem is the very thing they can't write. It must be agonising. And why poetry? You're not going to get famous, and you're really not going to get rich. The issue, as Kei Miller seems to indicate, is identity itself.

Having said this, one reason this particular scandal has caused such ructions is because Mack has used poetry (the question suggests itself, whose?) to gain a PhD, and a job teaching creative writing at the Open University. *Laventille* is her second book, and publication credits mean everything in academia.

She has also, through her 52 activities, betrayed workshop culture. Writers share their drafts in absolute trust, and she has stolen the only asset they have: their work. Facebook is a big thing in the writing and poetry communities. It's like the water-cooler at the most spread-out workplace in the world. Sheree Mack was part of this and it's both how she gained access to the 52 group and also why her case has roused such emotion. She has betrayed an awful lot of people who − even aside from those who really did − felt like they knew her. Some, loyal to her, have lashed out at Ira Lightman, accusing him of racism, asserting that 'what she's' doing' is 'more important' than small matters of intellectual property.

I asked Lightman how big the whole plagiarism thing is, in his view. Are we sitting on a sinkhole? He replied, 'I think it's a minor problem, but it's a problem. I wouldn't even say one per cent of poetry published in the UK is plagiarised. However, what the case of Sheree Mack shows is that one can progress quite far, that institutions are slow to act and quick to cover up, and that they have a tendency to protect their own.'

He added: 'I socialised with Sheree Mack, and shared a bill with her more than once, and I didn't spot any plagiarism. The poetry world functions on trust.' At the time of writing, he confirms that he is still looking for source poems for the ones Mack has not acknowledged, and is still very much finding them.

THE LINE

It is as if we were back at the *Théâtre des Funambules*, during the era of *Les Enfants du Paradis*, when pale-faced Pierrots walked a rope before stepping onto the stage. It was actually a tightrope set across the proscenium, in front of Harlequin's coat (the stage curtain). Actors who were not acrobats or mimes fell off the rope and were sent to perform far up backstage. So the word 'rope' was banned from the theatre and its use subject to a fine. One had to say 'line'.

Marcel Marceau, Foreword to *On the High Wire* by Philippe Petit

A book fell into my hands last Christmas Eve: a loan from a friend who used to be a circus performer. It is out of print, almost as hard to obtain as the condition it describes: *On the High Wire* by Philippe Petit, translated by Paul Auster, with a foreword by Marcel Marceau. The book doesn't mention Petit's famous walk between the towers of the World Trade Center, but focuses instead on the technique of wire-walking, great walkers who have mastered it, and the spiritual impulse and rigour of the walk. It is the most natural thing in the world to get ideas about how to approach the writing of poetry from these great silent masters. They are dedicated to the line, subjugated to the illusion, and dependent for their own lives on their discipline.

A poet is not going to die if his line is slack or unsupported. But his volition and his meaning — which are the same, for the duration of the poem, as his existence — will. The line must be taut, and strong enough to hold, and the grease left over from production must not be oozing out of its 'soul'. (Petit buys huge lengths of cable and leaves them out in the garden for 'several years' to become completely dry and weathered, then cleans them with gasoline. Elizabeth Bishop did the same with her poem drafts.)

It's not enough just to walk the line: the art depends on a daily familiarity with it. 'Whoever intends to master the art of walking on them,' Petit writes, 'must take on the task of seeking them out. Of comparing them. Of keeping those whose properties correspond to his aspirations. Of learning how to knot them. Of knowing how to tighten them. It is the work of a lifetime.'

Later he writes, 'If you want the High Wire to transform you into a high-wire walker you must discover the classic purity of this game. But first you must master its technique. Too bad for the one who turns it into a chore.'

Here I need to make a similar disclaimer to that made by Don Paterson in his two-part essay, 'The Lyric Principle', where he defines his subject, lyric poetry, as 'that aspect of the art that concerns itself to its music, i.e. to the patterning of its sounds.' Where Paterson says that 'language itself has a lyric basis and is itself a poetic system, and that poetry is merely the natural result of language placed under certain kinds of formal pressure and emotional urgency,' he is talking about one cross-section — sound, as expressed in vowels and consonants. We are occupying ourselves here with another of the almost limitless cross-sections available: the line. Clearly the line plays a different role in sound, concrete, 'innovative,' 'post-avant,' language and other poetries. But our working definition is still very broad, and ranges across styles and eras, and even widely differing sets of intentions. It includes, in part, many of the poetic styles listed above, and certainly applies to something like, say, Edwin Morgan's 'Siesta of a Hungarian Snake.'

The line is not the destination. Although its anchoring points — the nearest it has to a geography — are of the utmost importance, they are not the destination. They are more like the points of a compass. The real destination, in poetry as well as the Funambules, is what you do while you're up there. The line must hold you up so you can do it. Here is that snake poem in its entirety:

s sz sz SZ sz SZ sz ZS zs Zs zs zs z

A line of poetry, whether 'free' or 'formal' (more on that later), is made — crudely — of words and line endings. Words are made of meaning and sound. Meaning is made of dictionary definitions, association, history, etymology, and even — to some extent — sound. This can be based on onomotapeia, as Morgan demonstrates, or can be more expressionist, based on the principles in Paterson's essay — or both. (Some of us have varying degrees or types of synaesthesia, too, in which sounds and the shapes of letters, and the different kinds of meanings they combine to express, will be further bound up with, say, colour.)

The meaning in poetry flies higher (despite being, in Keats' words, 'loaded with ore'; it is packed light, with ore) than the meaning in prose: two sentences with identical meanings can mean vastly different things according to the choice of words and sounds. Sound is made of waves, which produce both noise and a physical effect on the body. These waves make patterns: openness and closedness, assonance and alliteration, rhyme, dissonance, rhythm, even a kind of melody, in cadence. As well as long and short syllables, words have different lengths according to their vowel sounds, use, and positioning in the sentence.

Rhythm is a patterning of relatively regular emphasis, of speed, pauses — which in poetry we call *caesurae* — and of the length of the line itself. We measure the most regular rhythms with metre. Metre is measured in feet of neatly-laid-out syllables, or by the number of syllables that are emphasised in a line. Some irregularity or substitution of the odd foot is permissible, even desirable, but if it gets too irregular it becomes free verse, which may have a defined, if loose, rhythm of its own. But metre by itself is not enough to organise a line, and free verse is not off the hook either.

Every line, every one of these assemblages of vowels, consonants, words, meanings, rhythms and counts and lengths and stresses, with its metaphysical bundle of meanings attached, has a beginning, a middle and an end.

The most problematical part of a line is the end, of course (which leads to the beginning of the next). Many poetry tutors don't like to discuss them at all; there is such a taboo on discussing this most personal aspect of poetry that mentioning it at all feels like crying "Rope!" in the Théatre des Funambules.

The poet Michael Donaghy used to say, "If you write with rhyme it's like walking into the room on stilts or a tightrope, saying, *look what I can do*! But if they can see it coming, you fall on your face and they'll laugh at you instead of admiring your skill." I'd like to add the line ending in general to his analogy. The end stop, the enjambment, the if, and, or but, the clever trick, the effects of rhyme, the carefully-styled hyphen, the repetition, the open ___.

If you use line endings clumsily you run the same risk of falling on your face. Either the reader should glide obliviously over your line ending and straight into the next line, or the jolt should provide some kind of *pleasure* that is inextricable from the *purpose* of the poem.

Pleasure is another concept that might need spelling out here. Poetry exists for pleasure. Like the frisson that must accompany the knowledge of certain death if one falls — imagine how Philippe Petit felt on a good day, say while he was wirewalking between the two towers of Notre Dame Cathedral — one of the chief pleasures afforded by poetry is the stimulation afforded by new combinations of neurons firing in the brain. Sound waves are physical, and brain activity is physical, because energy acts on our tissues: intellectual activity is mixed with sensory, and brings the same kinds of hormonal rewards (euphoria, for example) as physical activity. In his monograph *Wallflowers*, Donaghy wrote about the physical effect on your brain caused by merely mouthing the words while you read.

AS Byatt addressed this issue face-on in the *Cambridge Companion to John Donne*, extracted in the *TLS*:

> I came across a remark by a neural network designer about puns. Perhaps, this scientist said, we delight in puns because the neurone connections become very excited by the double input associated with all the stored information for two arbitrarily connected things or ideas. Perhaps we enjoy this excitement. It occurred to me, reading this, that complex metaphors produce infinitely more subtle versions of this excitement and pleasure. I started to think - to use a double entendre that is very pertinent - about the play on words, the play of light on a landscape, the mind at play. I know that this excitement is the primitive thing at the source of why I want to spend my life writing and thinking. I do not have a message to give to the world, I do not wish to seduce or persuade, I want to think as fast as possible, in as complex a way as possible, and put the thinking into verbal forms.

This is the source of the pleasure afforded by Morgan's Hungarian snake, with its progression from one childhood sound-meaning to another, via a playful observation on the Hungarian language, and wrapped up in a sight gag. (Also, note its completeness as a line. It floats complete on the page like one of those floating shelves from IKEA, needing no other visible support.)

In the world of the high wire they call the end points — both ends of the line — the anchor points, and walkers take great care where and how the anchors are to be placed. A line of poetry is no different. The end points need to be placed in such a way that the reader can get from one to the other, and nimbly down to the next, in the way the poet intends.

There are several different kinds of line endings, each carrying its own power, and its own risk of slackness. Blank verse is an elastic form about whose enjambments whole books have been written. If you've seen wirewalkers jumping or bouncing on their wires, you will know what can be learnt from a form like this:

> Best Image of my self and dearer half,
> The trouble of thy thoughts this night in sleep
> Affects me equally; nor can I like
> This uncouth dream, of evil sprung I fear;
> Yet evil whence? in thee can harbour none,
> Created pure. But know that in the Soule
> Are many lesser Faculties that serve
> Reason as chief; among these Fansie next
> Her office holds; of all external things,
> Which the five watchful Senses represent,
> She forms Imaginations, Aerie shapes,
> Which Reason joyning or disjoyning, frames
> All what we affirm or what deny, and call
> Our knowledge or opinion; then retires
> Into her private Cell when Nature rests.
> Oft in her absence mimic Fansie wakes
> To imitate her; but misjoyning shapes,
> Wilde work produces oft, and most in dreams,
> Ill matching words and deeds long past or late.
> Some such resemblances methinks I find
> Of our last Evenings talk, in this thy dream,
> But with addition strange; yet be not sad.

As with the rope, this blank verse of Milton's — where Adam consoles

Eve after her foreboding dream — is coiled of several strands, and cannot be broken without separating those strands. Milton used caesurae to punctuate and create variations of rhythm within the iambic pentameter. This allows him a great freedom with syntax, which simply serves to strengthen his line further and make it more powerful. His sentences take full advantage, with tumbling images and sub-clauses. If you read from caesura to caesura, you will find that often the 'line within a line' created by the two caesurae is itself a line of iambic pentameter:

among these Fansie next her office holds

frames all what we affirm or what deny

in this thy dream, but with addition strange

Milton was blind when he wrote *Paradise Lost:* he composed each section of 40 lines in his head overnight, and would dictate it to an amanuensis the next day. His family reported that if the secretary were late, he would be pacing up and down, furious, desperate to disgorge himself of the lines he was holding in his head. This metre was formed in the ear.

As well as sound and shape, lines contain intellectual, imagistic and emotional content; there are also a myriad of rhetorical purposes, ego trips and sheer cackhandedness to think about in analysing the line in contemporary verse practice. This essay is not long enough to deal satisfactorily with all these elements, so the list below is more like one of pet peeves — a guide for the unwary — combined with examples of excellence, chosen almost at random from my recent reading. The list runs down a spectrum of enjambment, beginning at the top with full sentences and ending at the bottom with particles so small they might be those .7mm bits of plastic they've discovered in the middle of the Atlantic.

First, there is the completely end-stopped line. This kind of line is rarely found in groups of more than two, but is employed to great effect in Chris Emery's poem, 'Carl's Job'.

> 'We need you to cope with all the little jobs,' smiled Carl.
> 'We want to make sure you target single losers, too,'
> 'Sure,' I laughed. *'I was very sad to hear about Verna.'*
> 'How the hell do you know about my wife?' asked Carl.
>
> *'I was the one who ran over her that time,'* I replied.
> 'You mean that time at Hennessey's; the time she died?' said
> Carl.
> *'Right,'* I said. *'The time she died; running off the verge.*
> *She kept her left leg twisting; it was a little strange.'* I smiled.
>
> 'What the hell do you want with me?' asked Carl.
> *'I've come to apply.'* I said. *'I want to work with you now.'*

The flat tone; length of the lines; the lame extra foot in each line, on top of what would have been roughly iambic pentameter; the presence of further full stops within the lines; the strange reported facial expressions: all work together to show us what the poet calls 'the scariest job interview ever!' The information is declarative, rather than descriptive: the few descriptions are more like something from a police report. There's no room for much else.

Then there is the line that ends on the end of a clause; this is much more common, because more flexible, but it operates in the same way, in units of knowledge. Often two lines make up a sentence, or unit, with a comma or semi-colon at the end of the first one.

In poetry, a unit of knowledge is an image — in Ezra Pound's definition, 'an intellectual and emotional complex in an instant of time.' Pound used this line to construct his pared-back two-liner, 'In a Station of the Metro'. This poem became the 1913 banner around which he rallied the Imagists: 'I wrote a thirty-line poem, and destroyed it because it was what we call work 'of second intensity'. Six months later I made a poem half that length; a year later I made the following *hokku*-like sentence.'

> The apparition of these faces in the crowd;
> Petals on a wet, black bough.

Today these lines seem almost quaint, with their capital initials, narrative quality and para-rhyme. But Pound was attempting something parallel to what painters at that time were doing: stripping the art down to brass tacks.

When discussing the unit of the line, even a century after Pound's image-poem, it is impossible to escape from the omnipresence of rhyme. It looms over us like the Post Office Tower in Bloomsbury, so gargantuan that we forget always to see it. Indeed, it is possible for rhyme to creep in where the poet isn't even aware of it. Used well, it has an amazingly galvanising effect on a poem.

Because rhyme is a kind of snapping-shut device for a unit of meaning, it is hard to resist the temptation to deploy the rhyme word at the end of a line. This is what our earliest poetry influences — the nursery thymes — do, and it can lead to a sort of tragic heroic couplet syndrome. Here, from the second stanza of 'The Rape of the Lock' (with spelling modernised):

> Now lapdogs give themselves the rousing shake,
> And sleepless lovers, just at twelve, awake:
> Thrice rung the bell, the slipper knocked the ground,
> And the pressed watch returned a silver sound.

Belinda still her downy pillow pressed,
Her guardian sylph prolonged the balmy rest...

This is the tendency that led Oscar Wilde to say, 'There are two ways of disliking poetry. The first way is to dislike it; the other is to read Pope.'

Frederick Seidel employs this device, too. Strangely, in his poetry it gives the impression that the flat-voiced narrator is concealing his feelings, not that he doesn't have any. It creates the same effect of an unreliable narrator as *Catcher in the Rye*, and a poignancy at odds with the poet's rather heartless reputation.

And when the doctor told me that I could have died.
And when I climbed up from the subway to the day outside.
White summer clouds were boiling in the trees.
I felt like falling to my knees.
Stand clear of the closing doors, please! Stand clear of the closing doors, please!

This is extreme usage (though note Seidel's internal rhymes, 'boiling' and 'falling' and the repetition of his line-beginning, 'And when').

End-stopped lines are more commonly used to construct the platform onto which a variation springs, in full spangle, to create colour and meaning, backflipping the reader to the next line, with *its* possibilities; or to bring a series of enjambed lines to a conclusion, like a flying trapeze artiste coming to land on the wire at last.

The line that ends on the end of a phrase, rather than a clause, begins to be, in normal usage, the contemporary line: a bit edgy, a bit risky, the judgement of which comes down more to a gut feeling rather than a rule. It will usually be mixed up with lines that break at the end of clauses: an amalgam of enjambment.

Take these two stanzas from near the beginning of Basil Bunting's Modernist masterpiece, 'Briggflatts':

Every birth a crime,
every sentence life.
Wiped of mould and mites
would the ball run true?
No hope of going back.
Hounds falter and stray,
shame deflects the pen.
Love murdered neither bleeds nor stifles
but jogs the draftsman's elbow.
What can he, changed, tell
her, changed, perhaps dead?
Delight dwindles. Blame
stays the same.

Brief words are hard to find,
shapes to carve and discard:
Bloodaxe, king of York,
king of Dublin, king of Orkney.
Take no notice of tears;
letter the stone to stand
over love laid aside lest
insufferable happiness impede
flight to Stainmore,
to trace
lark, mallet,
becks, flocks
and axe knocks.

The thing to notice here is how Bunting, while giving the illusion of 'difficulty', organises his images as neatly as if they were folded in a drawer. The rhymes don't announce themselves with flashy metre, they simply arrive, like rocks in a landscape. Nevertheless, each stanza is woven through with internal rhyme and para-rhyme

— elbow/tell her, shame/changed/same, stray/stays, mites/ delight, York/Orkney, Bloodaxe/becks/axe — and each ends on a rhymed couplet. The disintegration of the syntax into a list at the end of the second quoted stanza is not confusing, partly because it is clear *beforehand* what the list is, and partly because it is organised by rhyme, and the logic of the poem.

We can play a game with it, and re-break the lines in the way someone less skilful than Bunting might.

> Every birth a crime, every
> sentence life. Wiped of mould
> and mites, would the ball run
> true? No hope of going back. Hounds
> falter and stray, shame
>   deflects the pen. Love murdered
> neither bleeds nor stifles but jogs
>
> the draftsman's elbow.

What do we see? Orphaned words at the ends of lines, running to catch up with the ones on the line beneath before they get away. Sense harder to get at because of the unsympathetic breaks. Symmetries ruined, and edgy (but empty) rhythms created. 'True', at the start of New Line 4, echoes like the refrain in a 60s pop song. 'Falter and stray, shame' is a line too clotted even to falter, saved only by Bunting's prosody; the penultimate line is now trivial, and the final line portentous and reminiscent of Peter Greenaway. (If we were really going to do the thing properly we would loose it from its moorings and let it drift sadly on its own at the bottom, suddenly carrying on its own the dead weight of everything that has gone before. Oh, wait! There: done.)

After that there is the straightforwardly ambiguous

Postmodern ending, smack in the middle of a phrase, so that the relationship between the final word and the first one on the line below becomes pivotal for the poem's meaning. This kind of line needs to be crystal clear. In 'Pour' Philip Gross writes:

> Call it connecting
> one moment with another:
>   water-

> in-the-glass with water-in-the-jug,
> two bodies of water
>   and between,

>   this slick and fluted glitter...

If this isn't 'an intellectual and emotional complex in an instant of time' I don't know what it is; and — notwithstanding its indentations, broken compound, enjambments over stanzas, and lack of verbs — it is held firmly together by the visual imitation of falling water, and the sounds of its water: *connecting, another, water, water, bodies, water,* and the wonderful *glitter...*

There is a tension between the ending of one line and the start of the next. If the second half of an enjambed phrase changes the meaning of the previous line, in a way that doesn't add to the meaning of the poem, it misguides the reader, breaks the anchor point between the two lines and sends the reader flying through the air into the canyon (or water). This can happen if the poet ignores the fact that a word could be read as either a verb or something else: in this case, two words.

> So long as alluvial mud remained, and rotted
> wood, or rinsed white bones of crocodiles

Did the alluvial mud rot the wood, or rinse the bones of the crocodiles?

In the next example, we must first get past the fact that 'Sat' is being used as an adjective, to describe the state of the grandfather.

Sat on a dining-room chair he had turned
himself years before, he'd sip tea as I played

It's not that 'he' (implied) sat; it's that he *was* sat. Caught out once. Then the verb, 'turned', not only at first suggests a different meaning — that the grandfather had turned *around* in the chair — catching us out twice — but, even as we realise it is 'turned' as in woodworking, acts in the reading as if the next word ('himself') were the object of the transitive form of the verb. Caught out again: three strikes! And into the chasm we drop! There is even a possible reading where it could be said that he had turned the dining room chair *into* himself.

(This couplet also falls prey to a different problem: it has slipped unknowingly, in a poem that is not in metre, into a jaunty dactylic tetrameter. The mood of this metre is at odds with the mood of the poem, and nowhere is this jauntiness or metre repeated.)

There is another model, where the poet takes a figurative expression and breaks it in half. The reader reaches the end of one line, thinks it means one thing, and then discovers a split second later that in fact it means another thing. Done well, this can be a great device in a poem, adding a layer of meaning with economy and wit. Done badly, it means the reader has to go back, reread the first line, realise in advance what it actually is getting at, and then proceed, having gained nothing from the experience. This weakens the poem substantially, renders the poet an unreliable guide, and makes the reader feel — according to his skill and confidence as a reader — either annoyed, or as if the misunderstanding was somehow his fault.

And finally there is the utterly atomised line break, on a preposition or particle, or on a weak word intended to call the very notion of importance into doubt. This is the most dangerous kind of line break, partly because of its difficulty, and partly because of its ubiquity, as so many poets adopt it merely to break up something they think would have looked predictable otherwise, without understanding fully how it works.

Remember Petit's injunction to seek out your materials, get to know them, learn to recognise their properties at a glance? Ending on a preposition or particle creates a particular nervy effect, and operates as part of a system whereby the line is weighted at its first word — so the dying fall of the ending is a ruse, and the first word of the next line picks you up and tautens the whole thing again. In fact, the particle or preposition at the end of the line is what puts the weight on the start of the next line — so you'd better be sure it's really taut enough to sustain the tension this creates.

Highwire artists can write this line, and from the ground below they look as if they're floating. But in reality they are gripping on with toes of pure muscle.

Sharon Olds is the exemplar *par excellence* of a nervy, emotional, tense use of this kind of line-break. Putting the stress on the first word of the line below, it creates a sense of urgency as well as hesitancy, and disorients the reader, who then grabs for the emotional content as for a lifeline. In spoken delivery, this line can sound breathy, and lends itself to what we know as the Poetry Voice, full of portentous pauses, intended to alert the listener that something Important (and not normally audible in speech, because in fact based on a typographical construct) is happening. But on the page it races down to the bottom. From 'I Go Back to May 1937':

I see my father strolling out
under the ochre sandstone arch, the
red tiles glinting like bent
plates of blood behind his head, I
see my mother with a few light books at her hip
standing at the pillar made of tiny bricks with the
wrought-iron gate still open behind her, its
sword-tips black in the May air,
they are about to graduate, they are about to get married,
they are kids, they are dumb, all they know is they are
innocent, they would never hurt anybody.
I want to go up to them and say Stop,

Most of the lines here begin big, heavy, emphatic, and seem to lose
substance towards the end, tipping the reader onto the next line like
rain off the end of a twig — where the same thing happens again.
The punctuation (mainly commas) refuses to admit a stop for breath
until it's absolutely necessary, so the reader falls like a drop from
twig to twig until fairly exhausted. This is an effective technique.
On the other hand, aside from the shock and awe of the images —
the 'plates of blood', the tortured 'wrought-iron gate' still fruitlessly
open, the 'sword-tips' — it doesn't allow much room for anything
else much to be happening in terms of effect. This passage ends with
the word the poet wants to say to her young parents: 'Stop' — which
is exactly what the reader is not allowed to do.

Marianne Moore, who could not be much more different
from Olds ('tight, brisk,/Neat and hard as an ant'), renders this
device deliberate, precise, meditative. She uses it in aid of her (and
the reader's) eye, supporting a syllabic scaffolding of gossamer
lightness. 'The Mind is an Enchanting Thing' uses the preposition-
based line break to direct the traffic of our attention. Rather than
trying to be clever with us, she guides us almost as by the hand:

is an enchanted thing
    like the glaze on a
katydid-wing
    subdivided by sun
    till the nettings are legion.
Like Gieseking playing Scarlatti;

like the apteryx-awl
    as a beak, or the
kiwi's rain-shawl
    of haired feathers, the mind
    feeling its way as though blind,
walks along with its eyes on the ground.

This delicacy is achieved by a careful balancing of effects (including, potentially, a high Scrabble score). Line 2 ends on a preposition; in the next stanza, line 3 ends 'without', and in the next, on a new sentence 'It', and in the stanza after that, 'the'. Clearly line 2 in this poem is a place of doubt, or confusion and explanation, of pause before the big leap; where the reader is pointed on towards the main point, the image. But in every stanza lines 1 and 3, and 4 and 5, rhyme. This creates an element of rounding-off, which resolves the question formed by the dangling line-end above.

At the very start of the poem, the mind is enchanting, and then enchanted, 'like the glaze on a' — pause — then the surprise, and the image: 'katydid-wing'. It is the wing we are meant to notice, but the glaze, because we wondered briefly what it was on, retains its shimmering importance. And with that word 'subdivided' the poet shows us how she has made her image work.

The extract by WS Merwin that follows is, characteristically of him, anchored by syntax. There is no punctuation; Merwin's colloquial two-to-three-beat lines keep the poem well moored. This is a style of poetry best written by those who understand sentence construction, who are alert to all the possible meanings of a word.

Why did he promise me
that we would build ourselves
an ark all by ourselves
out in back of the house
on New York Avenue
in Union City New Jersey
to the singing of the streetcar
after the story
of Noah whom nobody
believed about the waters
that would rise over everything

Whether or not this is the kind of poetry that floats your boat, this is unquestionably the work of a poet lying down on the wire taking cups of tea. It looks easy, but it takes a great deal of discipline and care to be this simple.

There is a potential spill where he writes, 'that we would build ourselves', which could look like 'ourselves' was the object of 'build'; but the save is immediate: 'an ark all by ourselves'. The first, purely colloquial, iteration becomes an amplifier, characterising the speech of the small boy and symbolising Noah ('whom nobody/ believed') as a child (who has to ask again and again), and thus the child in all of us when dealing with issues of higher importance.

By the same token, the line break on 'after the story/ of Noah whom nobody' might look arbitrary, but it gives the following line anchors for its own full weight: 'believed about the waters.' Does the father believe about the waters? You might well ask.

I recently heard someone say they judged if the lines were working by how they looked on the page. If the poem looks okay, whatever that means, then the lines are working. This statement goes against the entire principle of the line, and what you're up there trying to accomplish. I'm not talking about concrete poetry, or poetry which has been written specifically with a particular shape in mind, like Morgan's snake. Sure, a poem should look nice on the page, but this will change according to the proportions of the typeface used, the kerning and general page layout and so on. I think it is more true to say that if a poem works, held together by its own internal tension in a state of organic tensile balance, it will tend to work on the page. The elements of this tension are listed above. Sound — that is, the sound the poem makes, and how it feels in your mouth as you make them — is absolutely critical.

This is the equivalent of understanding the rope's 'soul' — its inner core — just from feeling the outer layer with your fingers. If you really feel the sounds your words make, if you have tuned them as delicately as a violinist tunes his strings, you will never read out your poem 'metrically', with the stresses where they shouldn't fall. "Now IS the WINter OF our DISconTENT!" you will not say. In other words, 'looking okay' is a *sign, not a condition,* of success.

Philippe Petit's book contains a whole chapter on tricks and exercises which the high-wire walker must learn. These include walking backwards, doing comedy routines, wearing disguises and imitating characters or animals; incorporating other people or animals into the act; 'tricks with a Chinese umbrella or an Indian fan', dancing, jumping, taking tea, lying down. Once he is an accomplished high-wire walker, according to Petit (forgive the masculine), the walker keeps his low wire for practicing these exercises and inventing new ones, making them perfect, discarding the ones that don't work for him.

Silent and alone, he brings to the high cable everything he has learned down below. He discards the movements space will not support and gathers up the others into a group that he will polish, refine, lighten, and bring closer to himself.

The list of tricks, or exercises, a poet can perform on his or her line is also nearly endless. Some of them are even the same; see the above list and find even one you wouldn't like to see in a poem. 'Limits, traps, impossibilities are nothing to me,' writes Philippe Petit. 'Every day I go out to look for them. I believe the whip is necessary only when it is held by the student, not the teacher.' He describes practising in blizzards, in rain, on wobbly lines, in mismatched shoes, in wooden shoes, with people shaking the installation ropes. 'You must struggle against the elements to learn that staying on a wire is nothing ... Limits exist only in the souls of those who do not dream.'

MY LIFE IN TYPEWRITERS

First of all, if you're even going to think about measuring out your life in typewriters, you have to start with the belief that there is an ideal typewriter, the typewriter of all typewriters, and that it will change everything. It's the most beautiful typewriter in the world, whatever you think beautiful is. For some people that will be a large, mysterious old black machine with gold lettering on it and keys like old teeth; for others it's a sleek little slice of the sixties. It'll be green, or grey, or pink; it'll chatter to wake the dead or it will be muffled and sophisticated. The ideal typewriter has your perfect touch: crisp and snappy, or light and smooth. This typewriter has your name on it. Its keys will call out quietly to your fingers and no others. On this typewriter you will write faster, better than ever before; you will reach your Ur-space, the deep core of your purpose on earth.

My first recorded contact with a typewriter was when I was four. It was a story called 'The Tilty Fairy', about a fairy who was 'very old' (she was 24); I dictated it to my mother and she typed it up. At four years old I couldn't read, but I knew that a story your mother typed up was officially a story in a way that a story someone just wrote on a piece of paper could never be. It was the siren call of print.

She typed it on a classic American typewriter: a dull grey 1949 Royal Quiet De Luxe. She had been given it for her 15th birthday, which coincided with becoming the editor of the school magazine. It was the tool of her trade. One memorably hot, sweaty day, she trudged up the long hill to White Plains High School, lugging this machine that weighed almost a stone... and it stayed with her through school, and New York State University, and half her life.

I spent my childhood periodically climbing up on the big old wooden office chair to where that typewriter sat, on its big cluttery desk that was really a plywood door on two filing cabinets — a squat, dour machine, with glass-topped keys in the distinctive Royal shape cheerfully known as 'tombstone'. We kids used to type on it, finger by finger, writing our names or jokes or two sentences and then getting bored. Stymied. The thing was, you had to know how. The machine sat truculent in front of us like the piano downstairs, which only Dad and my little sister could make sing.

Then it disappeared. One day it wasn't there, and I can't even remember if I missed it. Years later it occurred to me that it must have been in 1977, when we moved to a smaller house. By that stage, it was all about the unlovely electric. Thinking about it, I must have asked, because Mom said — not just once, but enough times for me to remember — 'They're just uncivilised, I don't even know how we stood it'. So I begin to realise that even then I had some romantic feeling for the little stalwarts. I probably secretly wished I could type. I certainly loved our typewriter's case, which was a sandy-coloured tweed, like the old suitcase we also had knocking around. The typewriter case was the one that spoke to me of other worlds.

Mostly I preferred to write things in a notebook, like Harriet the Spy. I used a green or purple pen, wrote with a flourish, and drew pictures in the margins. By the time I had progressed to a tedious teenage Virginia Woolf phase, I was generally against everything, and especially electric typewriters. I had my own desk, the big old oak one my grandfather had written his sermons on, and I copied my poems out on it, over and over, in longhand.

This wasn't even weird yet. There were plenty of writers then who still wrote in longhand. Ted Hughes, for one, though of course I had no idea at the time, was dead against the typewriter. By using a typewriter, according to Hughes, you interrupted the inimitable spirit energy flowing from the core of your being, down your arm, into your hand and onto the page. He described this in a letter:

> Because handwriting is basically drawing of images (that's how graphologists read it — they decode the images in the various letters …) it engages not only the whole record of your psychological history (as your unique handwriting does) but it engages from word to word all the preverbal activities of your brain (as drawing images does), which then bring the (non-verbal) associative contribution to bear on what is being written about, and therefore help to determine the sequence of ideas and expressions, tones and rhythms etc...

Certainly there was more than a whiff of the mercantile and about a typewriter. It was easy to look down on them. I certainly looked down on anything mercantile, forgetting about poor Leonard out in the barn with the hand press. But we humans are also percussive creatures, and we embed the patterns of our bodies' movements into our being. We need our axes, our chisels, our hammers. Typing is atavistic, like beating drums; the result depends how and where you hit it. Humans were made to use tools, our hands are made for them, and our fingertips are fantastically sensitive. A typewriter is an ergonomic machine. In a real sense, with more bones and more moving parts than we have, it completes us at (or in!) our extremity.

Meanwhile, the little Royal lost to the sands of either time or the town dump, I was made to take typing at school. By this time the mystique of the career girl air traveller, purveyed by ultra-portables like the Empire-Corona Skyriter in its handbag-style case, was long gone. And because they were built to last, lots of people — like my mother — still had their dingy old 1940s models with keys named after a graveyard. Typewriters were brutal things, which had got girls out of the house and into the workforce, only to enslave us. The nostalgia craze spawned by *Mad Men* is an ersatz taste of what these machines used to mean in daily life. My mother and aunts were young working women in New York during the late 50s and early 60s, and regaled us with stories of the practically suicidal tedium, and the men.

At this point in the story your correspondent is a barefoot little feminist with unbrushed hair, no make-up, 800 books in alphabetical order, and subscriptions to *Verbatim: the Language Quarterly* and *Ms*. She has no idea what she wants to do when she grows up, and absolutely no idea how to go about doing it. Bizarrely for someone who will go on to be so utterly incompetent at admin, she has a little thing for index cards and filing cabinets, but also still writes everything out longhand using a green pen.

Someone suggested that I take typing. Maybe I had to, since I was failing geometry. Possibly someone suggested brightly that, as a writer, I might find it would come in handy — but by now everything really *was electric*, and I was against having to plug things in. I'd seen 'Network': I was as mad as hell, and I wasn't going to take it anymore.

So there I am, in a class with what feels like no content, with all the girls who are definitely going to be secretaries, and a couple of boys with pens in their breast pockets. The teacher has rather less personal charm than the slug lady in *Monsters, Inc*. It has not yet occurred to anybody to really lay it onto me that every job I might even plausibly want to get — for instance, journalist — as well as most of the ones I might actually get — will most likely require both typing *and shorthand*. It was my sister who got the piano lessons. She will go on to type 100wpm, her long nails like a monsoon on the keys, and will earn very good money for many miserable years as a legal secretary.

My typing class is a dead loss. The slug lady won't let me look. My high-water-mark is 18 words per minute. As it happens, my geometry teacher finds out that if he flunks me I won't graduate and he might have me back next year. So I pass geometry, and graduate, and forget even what kind of machine I was typing on.

When I was 20 I had to stay at my dad's for several months, doing temp jobs to earn enough money to come back to London. I made almost no money, because the main thing they needed people to do — the typing — I could not do. I did filing. I spent weeks in windowless basements removing all the paper clips and staples from huge insurance files, for microfilm. But one day the agency called. A client wanted a receptionist; it only involved 'light typing'; I could do that, couldn't I, the woman said encouragingly? She mentioned envelopes. I said, *well*, I don't type *fast*... and off I went into a wood-panelled office where I was left alone in a room with this — this —

I'd forgotten so much from that class. The first thing was all those formats and tabulation rules that were its actual content. Which side of a letter heading had the sender's address and which had the recipient's? How many rows apart? The margins, the double spaces between sentences. An hour or so later the nice man came to ask how his letter was coming on... He was tactful and kind; I think he even showed me how to do a letter; but two days later I was back in the basement.

The penny didn't drop, though. I merely found myself a couple of years later in that other sinkhole where young women go to be oppressed in the labour market. Retail. I was lucky to end up in a bookshop, where they used index cards and my encyclopaedic knowledge of publishers' imprints was actually of some use.

Cut to the computer age: I type pretty fast, with all the wrong fingers, and Word cleans up after me as I go. It sounds pretty good and I get praise for my typing, but I know I'm a fraud. In the computer age there is no such thing as a fraud. Nobody can touch-type. And everybody's handwriting is shit. In just a generation or two we have, as a world culture, stripped ourselves of the most basic manual literacy skills our parents and grandparents took for granted. But I've made it my own: my blog is in the top ten lists; I have over 3,000 followers on Twitter. I can make a website, I know about Search Engine Optimisation. I have apps.

Somewhere in here, while I'm owning the internet, I become aware that some people are 'typewriter collectors'. I'm not interested in those quaintly sad old stand-up Underwoods with all the ornate lettering and scary tall bodies, and crooked keys like sad teeth. To the extent that these are the typewriters that get attention, I don't connect myself to the phenomenon. Then a friend announces on Facebook that he has bought an Olivetti Lettera 35. I'm a successful blogger, I do social media marketing, I check my Twitter every couple of hours and take my laptop everywhere — and a year or two later I can still remember exactly what model he got.

Picture the scene. A day in 2014. I'm laid up on the couch with acute, painful tendonitis; they've given me crutches. As I lie there, I almost explode with a sudden, single, clear thought. I need a typewriter. I need it right now. I reach for the laptop, never far away, and look at eBay (bookmarked). It's worse than I even thought. I need *all* the typewriters.

When I finally did start writing (again) in earnest, after being put off it in my twenties by the fact that no one really wants you to write, it was almost like being four again. I wrote everything out longhand, copied it over and over, and worried about how to get it typed up. I thought of asking my sister, but of course that's like asking someone to knit you a jumper. Eventually I got a computer, because I had to — but even now I would print out my pages, go over them and mark them up, and cut them up to rearrange paragraphs and whole scenes. I used rolls and rolls of tape and ended up with long, stiff chapters, which I would then copy and paste in the software.

The typewriter shares one real virtue with handwriting, whether you compose on it or draft first in longhand. You have to make a whole new copy every time you edit. This repetition helps to deposit that work into your brain. And each act of going through the whole thing afresh brings new changes, even if you had already marked it up; the very bit we find tedious is what makes invention possible. 'Wordprocessing', as Ted Hughes wrote it, has always been about getting machines to do what we couldn't be arsed to. Actually working out what you were going to say. Remembering it. Paying attention.

Back on eBay, how could you possibly ever choose one of these machines over all the others? They're all so intensely beautiful. They seem to have faces. Some look like old sleek cars, some look like — well, like typewriters — intensely human. Unlike my last three laptops, these machines are 40, 50, 75 years old, and they still work. You don't have to plug them in. As I scroll down page after page of typewriters for sale, a thing happens.

In that single second, 30 years late, the penny drops. I'm going to need to learn how to type.

These days there are blogs and websites that list all the different famous writers and what typewriter they used. There are pictures of the writers with their machines. There's a man in America who collects the typewriters of famous people — Steinbeck, Updike, John Lennon — and keeps them on display in a little museum. I've spent many hours on the internet raking over this material, and it's struck me that, despite its reputation as a 'women's machine', most of the famous authors who pose like trophy hunters with their typewriters are men. Office typists worked on gigantic office behemoths; most of the men used portables, especially the really nippy, lightweight ultra-portables like the Hermes Baby. There's a picture of Thor Heyerdahl using a Hermes Baby on his lap aboard the Kon-Tiki. Doris Day just couldn't compete! The cachet of something like the Baby, which is 11x11 inches and 3 inches high, was partly that it was good for actual jetsetters and journalists. People who didn't have to pp their signature or get home and make the dinner. It pre-dated (and was smaller than) the Royalite with its aggressive career-girl marketing. It revolutionised typewriting, and it played to a perception — spoken, or unspoken — of *who* used *which* typewriter. Will Self, in our own era, has gone public with his beloved ultra-flat Groma Kolibri, a tiny (but heavy) East German portable, the ultimate gleaming boys' toy. (Kingsley Amis is pictured with an absolutely enormous Adler Universal 39, resolute in its unsexiness; Martin, the velvet-jacketed son, by contrast favoured the sleek Olivetti Lettera 32 — which pretty much only looks big when placed next to a Kolibri or Baby.)

Clearly, there were also women who used these chic models. Gamines. European women. A friend remembers going to sleep to the sound of her Polish dissident parents typing and smoking into the night; but I never saw anything like this in Hartford, CT. (And don't even get me started about the nicotine! These old machines are coated with it, inside and out — thick, viscous layers of it, like old ear wax.) There's no comparable Anglophone mythology about 'a woman and her typewriter'— no faithful sidekick, me and my horse, trail lore of the machine, no whisky and cigarettes till 6am. One of the only woman I'd have cared about back then who was photographed working on a typewriter was Sylvia Plath (and one of these was the sexy Olivetti Lettera 22) — but even she had a husband who disapproved of it.

Jack Kerouac wrote *On the Road* in three weeks, apparently typing about 100 words a minute, even on an uncivilised manual, on a continuous scroll of paper so he wouldn't have to stop. Paul Auster's Olympia SM9 has been made into a book, with paintings. Hemingway's various manly typewriters have been preserved after his death. William Burroughs and Joseph Brodsky were both pictured with Babys. Cormac McCarthy famously sold his battered Lettera 32, on which he'd written all his books, for $250,000 — and then his friend went out and got him one in better condition for twenty bucks. Larry McMurtry even thanked his Hermes 3000 in his Golden Globes award speech. It seems the writers with the famous typewriters were the guys.

It kind of reminded me what the problem had been in the first place.

Anyway, I went straight onto Facebook with this news, and almost instantly was offered the amazing gift of a little bright-orange Adler Tippa that my friend Pippa had used all through college. While I was delighting over 'Pippa's Tippa', my boyfriend had a Proustian moment: his big sister had had exactly the same model.

My need for Instant Typewriter was met by a 1959 Remington Quiet Riter listed on Gumtree by a collector called Peter, who has about 90 machines, including a world-class collection of about 30 Groma Kolibris. He constantly thins the herd by selling. "My girlfriend was starting to complain", he said, as my other half and I sat in his tiny kitchen in an ex-council flat in Battersea. The room just beyond was where he kept the typewriters, he said. It began to feel like an offstage character, full of teetering piles of cases and machines; little did I realise how soon my own living room would look like that. I typed a few random keys and tried the carriage return lever on the Quiet Riter.

Why was he selling this one?

He just smiled. "I have another".

My Quiet Riter is all busty-looking curves — it projects a sturdy, bosomy comfort — in a very classy dull green colour, with tiny gleaming dark green keys. It's built like a 1959 American car, and it bore this out when I had to carry it in its case. We forget the sheer weight of things, with all our plastics and silicon, zirconium and titanium and space-age fabrics and 3oz smart phones and our tablets that get thinner every year.

It was like a car again when I started typing on it — one of those big old invincible ones with seats you sank into, and acres between you and your siblings. Everything is authoritative: the paper slips in and the knob turns with a smart businesslike click, the carriage glides across the rails, the bell dings, the return lever is smooth and decisive. This Remington even has the best smell I've smelled on any typewriter. Leather, mechanics and time. It sounded deafening that first night, home alone with just the desk lamp on, typing gingerly in a little pool of light, but I know now that it earns its name. Its sound is clean and snappy, but with a discreet hush at the point where the key hits the platen and snaps back. This is caused by its 'noiseless' mechanism, a feature that was used on many typewriters with 'Quiet', 'Silent', or 'Noiseless' in their names.

Here's another thing we've deprived ourselves of, thinking it's an improvement, that our parents and grandparents took for granted: a whole world of sound. A world with no headphones, where cars made one noise and horses made another, where there were no emails and people had to talk to each other to get anything done, and if you sent a letter it would be delivered by a real person. The gate might creak, the doorbell might ring, the letter would fall on the mat and make a sound or you would unlatch a metal mailbox to retrieve it. People chopped wood and used sewing machines. Throughout most of history you could walk into the house and have a good idea where everyone was and what they were doing.

Typing on a typewriter is intensely physical: there are vibrations, the table moves, sounds reverberate inside the machine. You are joined in a physical project with the machine; your touch creates a physical impact on the paper. I found early on that I felt almost self-conscious, even sitting alone, to be making impressions on a piece of paper. You can't press delete on something that's already printed, and you can't sit there silently making no impact on the world.

And you have to learn to do it properly. For the first couple of months my fingers went between the keys, my typescripts were illegible, I sounded halting. I used the internet to learn how, by watching an old 1944 US Navy training film on typing technique. Lenore Fenton, a speed-typing champion, presented the film in a style that made my old typing teacher look like Julie Andrews. But things are different now; I'm old, and I like her tweed suit. I spent hours in front of Lenore, holding my arms and hands the right way, sitting up straight, trying not to look. When you have to apply actual pressure to the keys, it really is important to hold your wrists right. And your fingers.

There's a pianist called Christina Kobb who has learned to play the piano according to techniques from 200 years ago. 'It's hard enough learning how to play once', she said, in an article in the *New York Times*. 'I had to become conscious of every motion in my hands and fingers, things that normally I would do automatically, by habit'.

While modern players tend to hunch over the keys and hold their forearms nearly perpendicular to the keyboard, 19th century style dictated that pianists sit bolt upright. The posture prevented players from bringing their weight to bear on the keyboard, instead forcing them to rely on smaller finger movements. The elbows were held firmly against the body, with forearms sloping down and hands askew.

As Ms. Kobb became more fluent in this approach, she found that certain movements — jumping quickly between disparate chords, for example — became swifter and more fluid. 'The elbow against your body serves as a sort of GPS, so you always know where you are', she said.

Chords and scales sound smoother and can be played faster, Ms. Kobb also found, and dramatic pauses between notes — often a matter of physical necessity rather than of style — are lessened. The old style also allows the performer to be more discriminatory and subtle in choosing which notes to stress, Ms. Kobb learned, producing a performance that is subdued by today's standards.

"There's a different physical feeling to playing, as well as a different outcome," she said.

This feels remarkably similar to my experience of learning to type after years of using a computer.

Getting a lot of typewriters means learning about your own physical style. Each one has a personality, a reward for hitting the key that's all its own. I could write about typewriters the way Kingsley Amis wrote about drinks.

In due course I discovered a thing called the typosphere, a section of the blogosphere where people type out 'typecasts' and scan them in as blog posts. Some even use the red part of the ribbon for @mentions and #hashtags. They show pictures of their typewriters, including before-and-afters of a filthy or worn-out old machine transformed to a gleaming one. Fortunately, there are tireless typewriter bloggers out there researching the typewriter's mechanical, manufacturing and social histories, digging up photographs and factory details and old repair manuals and scanning them in.

On my budget, I was going to need to learn from these guys as well as Lenore. Starting with a 1949 Hermes Baby I got for a knockdown price from an antique shop in Chiswick, typewriters have been all about my hands. I used internet descriptions and photographs as my guide, and set about dismantling the machine screw by screw. It was years since I'd done anything that made my hands dirty. I'd read up: I had methylated spirits, cotton buds, a screwdriver, a paintbrush for dusting, and a torch in my phone. I was ready for anything.

Unless you buy them for three-figure sums from the person who has serviced and repaired them, all these machines come with immense amounts of old dust, congealed grease, cobwebs, bits of insect, larvae shells, leaves, seedpods, cigarette stubs, hairs, receipts, rust, debris from rotting soundproofing foam, and in one case an old Westlife CD inside them. They need serious cleaning. They are coated with nicotine. The nicotine is really a downer, I have to say. Everything is yellow, inside and out, and has to be cleaned using meths, electrical contact cleaner, penetrating oil, rust remover, cloths, rubber reviver, chrome polish... They come with stuck keys, broken tab controls, carriages locked into place, ink all over them, rusted-up joints, type slugs loose, missing feet, bent type bars, worn-out teeth in the escapement. I've had a couple of machines turn out to be a different colour from what I thought.

Several hours later the Baby was gleaming. Its crinkle-paint — a dark, wartime-looking grey — was shot with metallic flashes of light. Its keys shone. And it worked. The carriage was sliding smoothly. The keys all snapped pleasingly and their type slugs were free of caked ink. I had put it back together and was sitting there in a haze of endorphins and love when my other half arrived back from collecting his 12-year-old son for the weekend.

And thus it begins. "Say", said James. "How does one learn to operate this device?"

Pippa's Tippa, the little flat orange 1972 portable, has adorable, slightly springy keys, so your fingers are almost bounced from one to another like children on a mattress; it gets up a momentum and you just keep going. It has a solid flat bottom, so you can take it onto the couch or the bed. It's made of plastic — it was the nearest thing to a groovy typewriter in its day — so it's lighter than the metal ones, though it's beginning to go a little around one of its screwholes.

The 1955 Olympia SM3, a legendary machine, is so businesslike, so efficient and stern-looking with its gleaming chrome carriage ends and return lever, you feel as if *you* are Lenore. Like the Art Deco lobbies in New York when I was small, like teachers with suits and blue rinses and brooches, it's like secretly entering a world before I was born. Typing on this machine is bracing and kind of thrilling, and makes you sit up straighter — as Kingsley might say, like a swig of Scotch over ice.

One night I picked up a 1961 seafoam Hermes 3000 — the machine I'm writing this on now — from a lady at St Albans train station. It is a truly wonderful machine. Even its case is full of joy: pale green leatherette sides, cream leatherette front, neat black piping, and taffeta lining. I took it into the rather grim, unpopulated station café and opened it, and was in love. If pale green can be buttery, it is buttery. If a metal thing can look human, it does. The 3000 has a gorgeous rounded ribbon cover and big, fat green keys: there's something about the scale of them, maybe it's like being a kid again. Side-on, the front and back sweep up to the rounded top; it has an economy and also a gentleness of line surpassed in no other typewriter. So much sensuous pleasure in a machine designed for work. There in the café, it was the typewriter I'd never had all my life. I typed a page or two. The keys are smart and decisive but soft, and muffled, and the ribbon still even had some ink in it. It's as reassuring as the Quiet Riter. And it smelled like my school library. Lying in bed that first night, I suddenly had an almost physical image — the Hermes with its cool greenness, the touch and the muffled whock of its keys, the solid unflappable progress of its carriage, and the way it spoke to me as if I were the only person in the world.

I was amazed one day recently to find a cream-and-green two-tone Princess 300, a German machine (made by a firm with the appealing name of Keller und Knappich) shaped like an ultra-flat, but a bit bigger and more solid, and thus more wonderful to type on — sitting on eBay with no one bidding on it. Cleaned up, it looks like new. It's just an incredible machine, with snappy but effortless keys that seem to want to go all on their own. And it looks like a saddle shoe.

Another surprise is how quickly you get used to the sound of typing again. It's pleasant, reassuring, when someone else is doing it; lately my boyfriend and I love nothing more than waking up on a weekend morning to the sound of James already at it, typing out one of his cyborg novels. And when you're the one typing, you're somehow enveloped in a bubble of sound. Inside the noise of a machine like the Princess, you're somehow protected from everything else. You can think. It must be a bit what flying a biplane was like.

I can see now that the Royal Quiet De Luxe was the perfect gift for a serious-minded young girl. It's sturdy and studious and not in any way distracting. It is certainly not pink; this typewriter was not about reinforcing gender stereotypes. It's physically satisfying in its stone-coloured solidity, but surprisingly small compared to how it looked when I was eight. My 1950 model has a fast action and neat, green keys — approachable, but not trivial. A boulder that can write. The laptop my daughter did her GCSEs with is now, five years later, broken. Dead. This machine from when her grandmother was GCSE-age still works perfectly.

There are a lot of people with typewriters these days. It's not just a hipster thing. We're just people who got sick of everything talking to us the whole time, everything vibrating slightly, everything having an LED light. We love the ingenuity of mechanical things, and doing things with our hands. We remember when you could lift the lid and figure out how to fix things. We want to reclaim our generation's birthright of great industrial design.

We love that the typewriter does not — like the computer, or the TV before it — render us passive consumers, or confuse us with a lot of stuff that's beside the point, but allows us to be alone, unmolested. It invites us. It sits with us. It lets us think. It gives us back our solitude.

These are our beautiful machines, made by human hands for human hands, to help us write. And that's all they're for. Unlike almost all the people we'll ever know, our typewriters *want* us to write.

I picture the strange, confused girl I was, sometimes, curled up on the dirty old plaid couch in her room, with her manual typewriter — maybe an old Zephyr or Clipper — a secret confidante that she loves all the more for the fact that no one understands it. In this secret world of typing, there would have been no one telling her she was doing it wrong, or not to look. She would certainly have been spared the business letters. And she might have learned something. If I could go back in time and see the girl I was — and frankly, I'd love to give her a piece of my mind — I would give her some carbon paper in a nice folder and say, *learn to type, kiddo.*